RAISING CHICKENS FOR BEGINNERS

O. BANKS

THE COMPLETE GUIDE TO RAISING BACKYARD CHICKENS
QUALITY EGGS, SAFE, HEALTHY, AND SMELL-FREE COOP

© Copyright 2021 - All rights reserved.

The content contained within this book may not be reproduced, duplicated, or transmitted without direct written permission from the author or the publisher.

Under no circumstances will any blame or legal responsibility be held against the publisher, or author, for any damages, reparation, or monetary loss due to the information contained within this book, either directly or indirectly.

Legal Notice:

This book is copyright protected. It is only for personal use. You cannot amend, distribute, sell, use, quote, or paraphrase any part, or the content within this book, without the consent of the author or publisher.

Disclaimer Notice:

Please note the information contained within this document is for educational and entertainment purposes only. All effort has been executed to present accurate, up-to-date, reliable, complete information. No warranties of any kind are declared or implied. Readers acknowledge that the author is not engaged in the rendering of legal, financial, medical, or professional advice. The content within this book has been derived from various sources. Please consult a licensed professional before attempting any techniques outlined in this book.

By reading this document, the reader agrees that under no circumstances is the author responsible for any losses, direct or indirect, that are incurred due to the use of the information contained within this document, including, but not limited to, errors, omissions, or inaccuracies.

TABLE OF CONTENTS

INTRODUCTION

WHY RAISE BACKYARD CHICKENS? 1
THE INITIAL EXCITEMENT 2
CONNECT WITH OTHER CHICKEN KEEPERS 3
A BIT ABOUT THE AUTHOR 4
READY TO START! 4

1. IMPORTANT FACTS TO CONSIDER BEFORE STARTING THE JOURNEY

WHAT DOES IT TAKE TO RAISE BACKYARD CHICKENS? 6
THE BENEFITS OF RAISING BACKYARD CHICKENS 6
PRECAUTIONS TO CONSIDER 9
    What the Law Says
    When Chickens Become Pets
    Health Requirements
    Sanitation for Success
    Basic Maintenance
    Shelter and Security
    Chicken Chums
    Commitment

BE PREPARED FOR THE UNEXPECTED 11
THE EFFECT OF CLIMATE ON YOUR BROOD'S PRODUCTIVITY 13
THE NEXT STEP 13

2. THE IMPORTANCE OF PREPARATION

BRINGING YOUR FLOCK HOME 15
THE SPACE CHALLENGE 15
THE IDEAL CHICKEN COOP 16
    Locale
    Critter Proofing

INDOORS/OUTDOORS 19
SOME GREAT IDEAS FOR YOUR COOP 21
DO CHICKENS HAVE MANNERS? 23
    Hen and Chick Behavior
    Chick to Chick Behavior
    Adult Bird Behavior

FEATURES BEGINNERS LOOK FOR 26
SUITABLE BREEDS FOR BEGINNERS 26
    Buff Orpington
    Cinnamon Queen
    Dominique
    Easter Egger
    Hybrid—Speckledy Hens
    Leghorn
    Plymouth Rock
    Rhode Island Reds

THE NEXT STEP 28

HEALTHY FEEDING HABITS

WHAT CHICKENS EAT	30
Water Management	
Feed Management	
TYPES OF CHICKEN FEED	31
CHOOSING THE PERFECT FEED FOR YOUR FLOCK	32
FEED INGREDIENTS	33
THE BEST WAYS TO FEED YOUR FLOCK	34
Starter Feeds	
Feeding the Correct Rations	
Feeds Ideal for Growing and Developing	
Laying Rations	
Table Scraps	
Organic Feeds	
Emergency Feed	
Yummy Snacks	
The 90/10 Feeding Rule	
Feeding Mistakes to Avoid	
THE NEXT STEP	38

YOUR BROOD'S HEALTH AND FITNESS

COMMON HEALTH PROBLEMS AMONG YOUR CHICKENS	40
EGG-LAYING PROBLEMS	40
Egg Yolk Peritonitis	
Lash Eggs	
Soft Eggshells	
Egg Binding	
PROLAPSE	42
PASTY VENT	43
EGG EATING	43
DISAPPEARING EGGS	43
BLOOD ON EGGS	43
STRANGE EGG SHELL COLORS	44
ODD-SHAPED EGGS	44
DISEASES	44
Fowl Cholera	
Avian Influenza	
Fowl Pox	
Coccidiosis	
Newcastle Disease	
Salmonellosis	
MEDICATED FEEDS	47
INJURIES	47
CHICKEN FIRST AID KIT	48
THE IMPORTANCE OF LIGHTING IN THE COOP	49
THE NEXT STEP	49

UNDERSTANDING THE IMPORTANCE OF CHICKEN LITTER MANAGEMENT

THE SCOOP ON POOP MANAGEMENT	50
IN-HOUSE WINDROWING	52
PARTIAL HOUSE CLEANING	52
DROPPING BOARDS	53
DEEP LITTER METHOD	53
Signs That the Deep Litter Method Is Working	
WHERE TO BEGIN	55
REQUIREMENTS FOR THE DEEP LITTER METHOD	55
VALUABLE TIPS TO KEEP IN MIND FOR THE DEEP LITTER METHOD	55
ADVANTAGES AND DISADVANTAGES OF LITTER MATERIALS	56
WARNING	57
THE POTENTIAL DANGERS OF THE DEEP LITTER METHOD	58
THE NEXT STEP	58

ROUTINE IS KEY TO YOUR SUCCESS

DAILY ACTIVITIES	60
Water Check	

FEEDING	60
WHAT TO FEED YOUR CHICKENS	61
TREATS	61
FOODS TO AVOID	61
HOW TO FEED YOUR FLOCK	61
WHEN TO FEED YOUR FLOCK	62
WARNING	62
EGG COLLECTING	63
CHICKEN WATCH	63
WEEKLY ACTIVITIES	63
Coop Cleaning and Maintenance	
MONTHLY ACTIVITIES	63
Bedding Management	
Nesting Box Cleanup	
Waterer Sanitization	
Preparation for Weather Changes	
Sanitize the Coop	
OTHER IMPORTANT RECURRING TASKS	65
TIPS FOR FULL-TIME CHICKEN KEEPERS	65
THE NEXT STEP	65

THE IMPACT OF WEATHER AND TEMPERATURE ON YOUR FLOCK

PREPARE FOR THE FALL AND THE WINTER	67
TIPS TO KEEP YOUR BROOD WARM IN THE WINTER	67
Watch Out for Frozen Feed and Water	
Preventing Water Freezing	
Remove Wet Spots	
Increase Lighting for Egg Production	
What to Feed Your Chickens During the Winter Months	
Encourage Exploration	
FUN AND GAMES	69
Collect Eggs Frequently	
Ensure the Coop is Draft-Free	
Provide a Well-Protected Outdoor Space	
The Deep Litter Method	
Watch Out for Frostbite	
THE BREED AND AGE OF YOUR FLOCK	71
MOLTING DURING WINTER	71
TIPS TO KEEP YOUR BROOD COOL IN SUMMER	71
Good Hydration	
Body Temperature	

FEEDING CHICKENS IN SUMMER	72
CARING FOR CHICKENS IN EXTREME WEATHER	73
Hurricanes and Tornadoes	
Thunderstorms and Flooding	
THE PARTING SHOT	74

LAYING HENS AND EGG PRODUCTION

WHAT TO EXPECT	75
HOW TO IDENTIFY LAYING HENS	76
REASONS WHY HENS MAY NOT LAY	77
THE JOY OF COLLECTING EGGS	77
GOLDEN TIPS FOR QUALITY EGGS	78

CONCLUSION

REFERENCES

A SPECIAL GIFT TO OUR READERS

This gift will dive you deep into the diversity of chicken breeds, their behavior and all critical aspects you need to know before choosing your most favorites.

Along with this Helper, find nine amazing facts about chickens you did not know about! Let us know which email address to deliver to by going to:

www.otis.publishlight.com

INTRODUCTION

Hi! You've made a great decision to raise backyard chickens! Have you got everything organized and ready for this exciting new venture? Okay, so don't panic if you answered a shocked, resounding "No!" You've come to the right place to learn all there is to know about raising backyard chickens for beginners.

And, yes, in case you're wondering, I started just the same as you. I wanted to know more about these fascinating, productive, and sometimes crazy birds. Soon, I developed a keen rapport with my brood, and, as a result, I've become pretty adept at communicating with my delightful, feathered friends.

Or at the very least, I've become so in tune with my hens that I notice things about their behavior that leads me to understand when they're hungry, thirsty, sick, playful, broody, or just plain having a "bad-feathered" day.

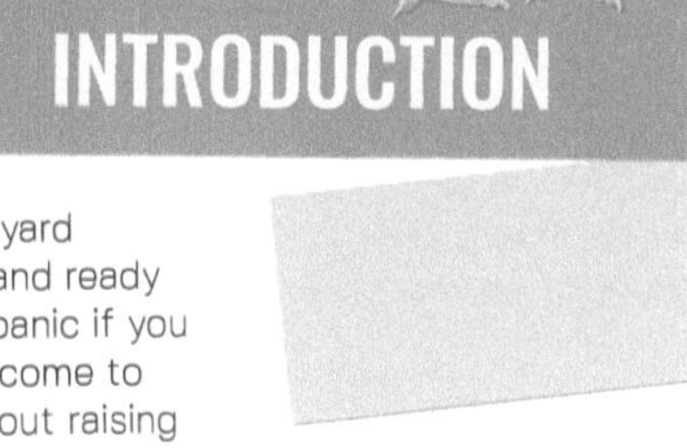

WHY RAISE BACKYARD CHICKENS?

Chicken keeping has become one of the critical elements of self-sustainability, and although you may feel somewhat overwhelmed by the plethora of information and advice on the subject, rest assured that you will find plenty of support on these pages.

Apart from soothing the farming instinct you may have, raising your flock of chickens has many positive aspects. Gathering delicious, fresh eggs for breakfast certainly is one of the compensations for your efforts. Plus, displaying your flocks beautifully colored provisions in a basket on your kitchen counter is a daily reminder of the usefulness of these wonderful birds.

Keeping chickens is a great way to teach children to help take responsibility for caring, feeding, and cleaning up after their pets. The kids will also learn about the natural life cycle of these birds and how they grow.

Provided the laws in your local neighborhood allow, raising chickens in the yard brings a bit of rural life to your doorstep. There is little to beat that farm touch for adding the glamour and interest of a small brood of chickens to your garden.

Not only are these feathered creatures pretty adaptable, but they're also a valuable, organic tool in keeping ticks, harmful bugs, and pesky critter populations down. Chickens make excellent pets. Despite some hens being manic and mean, the majority are delightful, intelligent birds that respond well to positive interaction with their people.

Watching your chickens play out their daily routine can be a very satisfying experience. Their uncomplicated approach to life may have a calming Zen effect on your nerves after a busy day at the office. Besides providing nutritious food, these feathered members of your extended family are likely to bring you great satisfaction and joy (Frame, 2010).

THE INITIAL EXCITEMENT

As with all things new, the excitement and enthusiasm of starting your home poultry-growing venture may begin to wane when you realize the initial setup effort needed to raise backyard chickens successfully. However, don't let the extra work dampen your spirits. Take it from me; raising chickens is one of the most fruitful and, not to mention, a fun pastime on which you can embark (Price, 2014).

The Plan
Your first step is to have a plan. Choosing the best breed of chickens for your needs is an excellent place to begin. Poultry comes in different sizes and colors. The standard breed is often the best as these birds usually easily adaptable and produces good-quality eggs and meat.

The Number of Birds
Determine the number of birds you want in your flock. This quota is vital when planning the coop. A good starting benchmark for beginners is between four and six chickens. Start small, and as you become more adept at raising your poultry, you may want to expand your enterprise.

The Budget
Remember, chicks grow into adult birds, and as they grow, they eat. Create a budget to help you stay on track with feeding, nesting, and essential caring requirements.

The Supplier
Please use a reputable supplier for your chickens, preferably a well-known and trusted hatchery known to be free of pullorum-typhoid, a combination disease resulting from *Salmonella* **pullorum** and fowl typhoid, discussed in greater depth in chapter four. For the most part, these diseases have been eradicated in the U.S. However, because it still exists in other parts of the world, especially in Central and Southern America, vaccination against the diseases is

essential to protect chicks' livelihood. The condition is passed from the hen to her chick through the egg, and high chick mortality results in areas where there is inadequate or no testing.

The chicks should also be vaccinated for coccidiosis and Marek's disease, also discussed further in chapter four.

The Brooder

Prepare the brooder to keep your new tiny chicks warm and draft-free. Essentially, this structure should consist of a completely enclosed unit, preferably with curved sides to avoid the chicks crushing each other into a corner when they cuddle together. The brooder requires a solid floor onto which you can spread suitable dry bedding. Each chick needs about three square feet of floor area during their first six weeks.

A heating lamp is essential to ensure a constant temperature of 90 °F during the first week. Reduce the heat by five degrees weekly until it reaches 55 °F.

The Coop

As with all livestock, housing is one of the most important things to consider. Where will your chickens live? Leaving these birds to roam free in your yard is unwise. Apart from the devastation of your dog eating your flock, other visiting predators may also become a problem. You don't want to lose your investment overnight!

Feeding and Water

Chickens are notoriously thirsty birds, so a constant supply of clean, fresh water in easily accessible water-tight containers is essential.

Added to this, chickens appear to be desperately starving most of the time. Fresh, good-quality grain should be laid out for your flock twice a day. This food can be placed in shallow trays or spread on the ground. Because these birds also naturally forage and scratch for grubs, seeds, and other edible items, you should prepare a safe area for your poultry to carry out these habits.

Two to Three Years Maximum

Your chickens can each give you up to two years of egg production before they begin to eat you out of house and home. After that, your birds become a useful food source themselves. However, if your flock is viewed as pets, no doubt your choice will be to keep caring for unproductive birds until natural attrition occurs.

CONNECT WITH OTHER CHICKEN KEEPERS

When starting on your new venture, consider reaching out for help and support from other chicken keepers in addition to surfing the net for information, forums, and heaps of valuable resources.

In your first years as a chicken keeper, you'll inevitably have questions. One excellent option is to turn to the vast world of information, and that would be the Internet. There are outstanding online resources, forums, and communities for chicken keepers, and by talking to people virtually, you can source from an endless pool of information and experience.

However, don't underestimate the power of local connections, too. Get to know other backyard chicken keepers in your area that offer advice and support one another. Some towns have a meetup group, where they do egg-themed and chicken-themed potlucks. You can learn a great deal about chicken keeping from these informal chats with other sustainability enthusiasts.

Local resources will also come in handy when your birds get sick, need care, or require veterinarian recommendations. It's also a forum to simply swap stories and buy and sell new birds (Omlet, 2004).

A BIT ABOUT THE AUTHOR

Otis Banks is an author dedicated to teaching techniques, knowledge, and the tools necessary to help newbies and more advanced individuals in poultry keeping. He combines both past and new issues to consider when embarking on chicken growing. Currently resident in Canada, Otis spent part of his life in Europe, Asia, and Africa, where he has been involved in chicken growing since the age of seven.

Otis is an authority on the subject of raising backyard chickens. Not only does he have a strong passion for raising poultry and chickens in particular, but he has also accumulated significant knowledge and experience in this field since his early years, which has helped him and his family thrive in poultry growing.

In writing this book, the author hopes to share his passion for poultry and his valuable experience and knowledge with others who are either considering raising poultry or who have already made a start and would appreciate further tips and hacks for a successful, productive brood.

READY TO START!

Without any further "peeping and clucking," let's get down and dirty as we explore the hard work, diligence, and excitement of raising your very own brood of delightfully noisy, healthy, and productive chickens.

1 IMPORTANT FACTS TO CONSIDER BEFORE STARTING THE JOURNEY

Though excited at the prospect of being a beginner chicken keeper, you may feel a little apprehensive about how to raise your chickens successfully. Don't stress. This chapter gives an in-depth overview of the requirements for starting your backyard chicken raising venture.

Raising chickens in your yard may appear to be the "in thing." Friends, family members, and many of your social media contacts are likely to show interest in your new venture. Some may offer you advice, while others may wonder why you would want to go to so much trouble for a small flock of chickens.

When you embark on the fascinating journey of raising backyard chickens, you will discover this hobby is not only fruitful and lots of entertainment, it's also a great learning curve for the kids and family.

Although the road to raising yard chickens can be somewhat steep and rocky at times, it's a worthwhile and rewarding hobby that brings the entire family heaps of fun and laughter. There will be some tears, too, as not all your tiny chicks will survive. Under normal circumstances, in which you have made a good provision for these little birds, the survival rate should be about 80%. There is, however, the possibility of unexpected health issues or the potential loss of flock members to the overzealous family dog or unpredictable predators!

WHAT DOES IT TAKE TO RAISE BACKYARD CHICKENS?

You need enthusiasm and a sense of adventure, for starters. Chickens wake at dawn and begin to get quite noisy if you don't hurry to let them out of their coop. If being an early riser isn't your thing, you may want to consider investing in an automatic coop door opener that can be set for sunrise. Otherwise, you'll just have to "rise and shine" and open up so that your chickens can stretch their legs and begin the day with their usual enthusiasm for life. Added to the noisome, warm welcome you get each morning, which is like unadulterated soul food, you get to collect newly laid eggs for breakfast. What a way to start the day!

Chickens, like most other pets, need a lot of attention. These birds respond well to the constant care and enjoy being around people. It doesn't take the chickens long to realize who brings their daily rations. Pretty soon, they will squawk, screech, and cluck with growing enthusiasm when they spot you coming toward the coop. However, if your chickens feel neglected, they may stop laying eggs or even become a little nasty toward you.

Neighbors, friends, and family members may wonder why you would embark on having a backyard mini chicken farm. For those of us who keep chickens, it's a no-brainer. However, in answer to the usual questions about your choice to raise chickens in your yard, here are some excellent reasons below (The Happy Chicken Coop, 2015).

THE BENEFITS OF RAISING BACKYARD CHICKENS

Raising backyard chickens is not only an exciting opportunity to extend your pet family, but it's also a valuable tool to learn about poultry and discover the satisfying upshot of having fresh eggs and meat right on your doorstep. Added to the fun of interacting with these quirky, sometimes eccentric birds, chickens have an amazing way of creeping into your heart.

Sustainability

With the cost of living continuing to skyrocket, many families have opted for becoming increasingly independent and self-sustainable. One of the best ways to serve this purpose is to raise chickens in your yard. Expect each hen to lay an egg a day, depending on the breed. Some breeds will produce eggs three to four times a week.

Besides, birds exposed to plenty of glorious sunshine, tasty bugs, fresh greens, and good-quality grain produce excellent eggs. It's usually only during the winter months they'll need grain and seeds. Plus, for those generous chicken breeders, mealworms make an added delicious, nutritious morsel for your hungry feathered beasties.

It's difficult to explain the sense of pleasure you'll experience when you stroll down to the henhouse to collect fresh eggs for your breakfast. There's no denying you'll feel secretly pleased with yourself for having embarked on your mini chicken farm. There's also that sense of knowing you're making an effort to feed your family without leaving the house to do the shopping. The added benefits of gathering eggs from your poultry are that you know their source and that the birds are cared for, properly raised, and well-fed. More than that, you don't commercially support birds and eggs raised on battery cages (Katherine, 2019).

Raising Chickens for Eggs or Meat

When you start, consider egg-laying

chickens. However, as you become more confident in raising your backyard brood, you may want to think about meat chickens.

Several suitable meat breeds will do well by being pasture-raised, while others grow more quickly in less space because they don't require as much exercise as their egg-producing sisters.

Culling the older egg layers is a meat option for birds that are no longer productive. These birds can be used to make tasty stews and nutritious bone broth.

Irrespective of your choice of breed for egg-laying or meat production, no store-bought eggs or chicken meat will taste as remotely delicious as your home-grown variety (Katherine, 2019).

The Pest Control Brigade

Chickens are the most amazing bug spotters. Their beady eyes don't miss a single potential, tasty morsel. If you allow your poultry to run freely in your garden, you'll never have to bother about pests that annihilate your crops. However, chickens are particularly partial to fresh vegetables and newly sprouting buds, so they too can cause a lot of damage to crops.

A great solution to pest control is to allow your feathered family to run free in the garden at the end of each season when crops are dying off. These busy, attentive little birds will cultivate the soil and eradicate the bugs hidden beneath its surface while disposing of fallen fruits and decaying vegetation. In this way, fewer bugs survive to bother you the following season because your diligent chickens have gobbled these pests.

As a conscientious chicken keeper, you may want to try collecting grubs, bugs, and tomato hornworms in a bucket while you garden. These delicious morsels will make your chickens dance with enthusiastic delight. Then, you can sit back and watch as your chickens scramble and jostle for every tidbit they can get their greedy beaks around. They'll love you forever! (Katherine, 2019).

Producers of Excellent Fertilizer

Chicken poop is rich in nitrogen, phosphorus, and potassium and makes a highly nutritious garden fertilizer. The manure can be composted and added to the lawn, flowers, fruit trees, and vegetable gardens.

You can dispose of the spoiled chicken coop bedding (straw and sawdust) by tossing it into the compost heap for added soil support.

Well-matured compost laced with copious amounts of good-quality chicken manure can be traded, sold, or simply used in your garden (Urquhart, 2016).

Remember, chicken manure needs to mature and break down before using it in the garden. Fresh manure can damage plants and burn the roots. So, like all things good and worthwhile, mix the chicken poop into your compost heap, which you'll turn every two to four weeks. The heat generated in the center of the compost pile helps convert the chicken manure into potential gardening gold. After a few months, your compost is ready for use, and your garden will flourish as a result!

Natural Garbage Disposal

Chickens love the excitement of having leftover greens, salad, rice, peels, nuts, seeds, and veggies tossed into their run. They're also partial to most garden weeds and will astound you with their fierce, intense concentration when eating these snacks. Often, how the birds attack these edible gifts may give you the impression they're starving! However, if you discover anything about these intuitive little gannets, you'll know they simply eat whatever they can when it's available. That's all good and well because the more nutritious the food, the better the quality of their eggs. It's a win-win situation all around (Urquhart, 2016)!

Low Maintenance, High Yield

Unlike many other types of livestock, chickens are easy to manage. The initial planning, preparation, and building of a secure chicken coop will take you time and effort. After that, you'll discover raising chickens is a breeze.

Change their water and food each morning when you open the coop. Around mid- to late-afternoon, the chickens should be fed for the second time and given fresh water. Early evening in summer and a little earlier when the weather begins to cool, your poultry should be closed into the coop for the night.

You should routinely clean out the coop and replace the chickens' bedding. Check for splintered struts, dampness, or any signs of damage. Make repairs as soon as these are needed. Also, check the perimeter fencing of the run and make repairs where needed. This security check will ensure chickens don't escape and potential predators don't gain access to your flock when you least expect it (Urquhart, 2016).

Entertainment

In all likelihood, you will spend a lot more time with your chickens than you may have at first thought possible. There's little to beat the enjoyment of watching chickens going about their daily routine. These feathered additions to your family are among the most entertaining and exciting creatures you can own. Their silly antics, fluttering, and jumping in crazy chicken dance style will have you in hysterics.

The Learning Curve

The learning opportunity for the whole family is an exciting addition to raising your yard chickens. You will learn about the chickens' life cycle and develop a sense of responsibility and care toward these sweet, feathered creatures (The Happy Chicken Coop, 2015).

Chickens adore taking dust baths that shower their feathers with grit and soil to dislodge mites. Sometimes, when one bird starts this activity, several others follow suit. It's best to step back until the dust has settled; otherwise, you too will be coated in grime!

Your feathered brood members can become quite chatty, clucking and crowing back at you when you mimic their sounds. There will be many times that you may wish you could understand "chicken speak," if for no other reason than to hear the comments these hilarious creatures might be making about their fellow flock members.

Family Members

Over time, chickens can form quite a strong bond with a family member. A neighbor's son, Calum, loves the two plump speckled California Gray chickens that were the firstcomers to their coop. Aptly named Betty and Bella, these two birds respond to the boy's greeting with clucking and head dipping. As soon as Calum enters the run, the birds hurry to him, doing their chicken dance as a welcome sign. Then, they settle down onto his lap, each pushing the other to gain the best spot while crooning with contentment. Admittedly, Calum always brings them a special treat, so it makes you wonder if the chickens' behavior is a sign of genuine affection or just a clever, manipulative maneuver.

Mindful Meditation

Strange as it may sound, watching chickens go about their daily business can have a hypnotic effect on your mind and soul. You may find quiet contemplation of these birds brings you to the point of intense peace where you become aware of every sound they make. The experience may have a profound effect on you. It may bring you to realize the importance of spending quality time with not only your flock but also your family (Urquhart, 2016).

PRECAUTIONS TO CONSIDER

Now that many of the positive aspects of raising your poultry brood have been discussed, there are several precautions you should keep in mind. To ensure that you succeed in raising backyard chickens, consider the following essential aspects below before you embark on your exciting adventure of becoming a chicken keeper (Johnston, 2018).

WHAT THE LAW SAYS

First off is, of course, the legality of raising chickens in your yard. Check with your local zoning office or city hall for a copy of the rules that apply to raising poultry in your state. Keep a copy of these rules handy in case there are unpleasant issues with neighbors.

The rules will give you essential details of the number of chickens you can keep regarding the size of the available plot of land. It will inform you if you need a permit and if regular health inspections are needed. You'll also find information about whether you can keep a rooster.

Agriculturally zoned land is ideal for keeping chickens and other small livestock. Commercial and residential zones are likely to carry more restrictions, so, do your homework before you set out to stock your coop.

There appear to have been some changes to the laws in several states in the wake of the increased interest in raising backyard chickens (Omlet, 2004). However, you may be required to sign a permit to go ahead with your plans to become a backyard chicken keeper. Do whatever is necessary, and you'll be rewarded with the most incredible experience of your lifetime.

Noise

The noise is often the most significant drawback, especially when it comes to neighbors who may not show quite the same enthusiasm for chicken keeping as you. So, apart from following the ordinance in your state (if they allow you to keep chickens), make friends with your neighbors and offer them fresh eggs every once in a while.

Raising chickens will increase the noise level on your property. Contented chickens are pretty quiet as a rule, but the odd spat over territory or food can cause irritable behavior and unpleasant squawking. Also, if you own a rooster, you can toss your alarm clock out as you'll be awakened daily by raucous crowing just before the sunrise!

Smell

All pets smell from time to time, and chickens are no exception. However, if you manage the coop cleaning routinely, the smell shouldn't reach unpleasant proportions. Chicken manure has a peculiar odor which many people find offensive. To avoid any unpleasant altercations, strategically position your chicken coop to ensure the prevailing wind does not waft the smell toward the neighbors. To keep the smell of raising chickens at a minimum, keep the chicken coop and run free from manure buildup (Omlet, 2004).

Once again, it may only be the neighbors who find the odor offensive. After all, you may not notice the smell because you have grown used to living with and taking care of your feathered family. If your backyard chicken enterprise generates enough compost to share, offer the neighbors some for their garden. In no time, you'll have won their hearts, and it may not be long before they too join the chicken keeping clan!

Sufficient Space

Like any animals, your chickens need space to live, grow, and thrive. Bear in mind that chickens need plenty of room to roam and explore. Those birds that are free-range need a safe area that's protected by predators. In urban areas, you're unlikely to have a permit to allow your flock to roam free. So, before embarking on your poultry venture, you must ensure enough space for a secure, well-ventilated, and safe cage and coop. Generally, the enclosure, which is where your hens will spend their nights, is attached to the fowl run. Chapter two discusses chicken housing facilities in greater detail.

WHEN CHICKENS BECOME PETS

As mentioned before, chickens can become adorable little pets, each with its unique, quirky personality. Some are shy, while others are curious, playful, or affectionate. There will be an exceptional pet among your flock for each family member, guaranteed.

On rare occasions, chickens have forged strong bonds with other family pets. An example of such a relationship is a chicken keeper's dog that is making a connection with the rooster in their flock. The two animals can become inseparable and wander all over the garden together. They can often be found napping in a patch of winter sun, with the rooster or the chicks snuggled against his furry friend's neck.

Be warned! If you intend to raise these birds for eggs only, there shouldn't be a problem with the bond the chickens may form with you and your family members. However, if the birds are being raised for meat, it would be best not to become emotionally attached to any chickens regularly culled (The Happy Chicken Coop, 2015).

HEALTH REQUIREMENTS

Chicken droppings attached to your flock's feathers and feet may carry *Salmonella*, which can cause serious illness. It's best to keep your hands away from your face while working with your brood, the coop, and bedding. Always practice good hygiene and wash your hands well after handling your poultry.

As with all pets, health care is essential for their prolonged life, comfort, and well-being. Chickens can become sick or injured. Most common illnesses include a prolapsed vent, bumblefoot, respiratory problems, and mites. There's more information about these ailments and their treatment in chapter four.

Now and then, chickens can bully each other, causing injuries that may require professional care. If these injuries draw blood, you may need to remove the injured bird to avoid it being attacked by the rest of the flock.

As your flock ages, egg laying will taper off. The average chicken can live to the ripe age of eight to 10 years. Their egg productivity is usually between one to three years. The decision will need to be made whether the aging chicken becomes dinner or is left to live out its life in the coop (Urquhart, 2016).

SANITATION FOR SUCCESS

Chickens need to be kept clean, and their coop and bedding should be spotless, free of decaying manure, food, and other unpleasant matter. Clean, fresh straw and pine needles make ideal bedding for your brood. However, avoid using cedar sawdust, as the oil can be toxic to chickens.

Young chickens are susceptible to health risks, so ensure you keep their living and sleeping areas spotless. Disinfect all building materials, bedding, and feeding equipment before you introduce your chicks. Thorough weekly cleaning of the chicken coop is essential to maintain a healthy flock (Urquhart, 2016).

BASIC MAINTENANCE

You must be prepared to shovel manure throughout the year. It's not only great exercise but excellent for the lush growth of vegetables and plants in your garden.

Besides keeping the coop and chicken run clean and in good condition, chickens need plenty of fresh water and good-quality food in the form of grain and vegetable matter. They also need the grit to help with their digestion.

SHELTER AND SECURITY

Depending on the state you live in, your flock needs adequate shelter against the heat and cold. They need a dry, cozy, safe area to sleep. Some chickens prefer perches on which to sit, though these are not an essential requirement.

The chicken coop should be totally waterproof and sufficiently sturdy to withstand an onslaught from potential predators in your area.

All chickens love to run, scratch the ground, and bask in the warm sunshine. Don't overcrowd your coop. Make sure there's sufficient space for your chickens to move around freely.

The coop may need to be brought indoors during severe winters. However, if it's a well-constructed, waterproof coop with plenty of clean, dry bedding, the chickens will crowd together at night to generate extra warmth (Urquhart, 2016).

CHICKEN CHUMS

Chickens are intensely social birds that enjoy each other's company. They love to cuddle together when the temperature drops and can often be seen playing and jumping together outdoors in their run. Solitary birds often die from loneliness, so consider investing in four to six chickens to start.

COMMITMENT

Taking on pets of any kind involves committing to care for their needs. At times when you're tired or disheartened, you may find yourself wondering why you embarked on this venture. However, if you stay committed, the rewards far outweigh any of the challenges. Remember, some chickens can live for eight to 10 years, so you're in for the long run (Whisperer, 2018).

BE PREPARED FOR THE UNEXPECTED

For the most part, keeping chickens is an easy and rewarding hobby. However, there will be times during your journey with your chickens when you need to be the emissary of life and, on occasion, death.

Though there are some health and safety issues beyond your control, your flock's safety is essentially your concern and responsibility.

As with all pets, your chickens rely solely on you for their welfare and safety. With this fact in mind, you need to be as well-prepared as possible to deal with a wide variety of chicken-related issues. These may be as simple as a fussy bird that won't eat alongside her sisters, severe stress, injuries from chicken battles, malformed eggs, and productivity problems. Whatever the case, like any good parent, you'll step up, armed with your chicken first aid kit, advice from fellow chicken keepers, and your common sense to deal with the challenges of raising your backyard flock.

Sudden Death

When a chicken suddenly drops dead for no apparent reason, the responsibility of this unexpected and unpleasant event can leave you wondering what you did wrong. In most cases, you may not have done anything to promote the premature passing of one of your flock. Awful though the event will make you feel, know that nature has a way of naturally culling the weakest animals and those that are ill. Be aware that the dead chicken may have had a disease that could potentially affect the entire flock. If in doubt, seek advice on what to do to protect your other chickens from a similar fate.

Undue Stress

You aren't the only one who suffers from worry and stress. Surprisingly, chickens are susceptible to stress due to temperature changes, overcrowding, unexpected changes in their environment, and traveling without adequate water and care. Therefore, the bottom line is to reduce the stress in your flock so that you can all live a long, happy, and productive life.

Predators

There's also the ever-present danger of flock members falling prey to predators. Among these beasts of prey are foxes, domestic dogs, raccoons, and weasels attracted by the smell of the flock and the inviting clucking, squawking, and cheeping.

Chickens can even fall prey to lice and mite infestations that can seriously affect their health and well-being. It's therefore essential that you prepare secure, safe, well-maintained housing for your flock.

Other Challenges

Besides your best efforts to keep your chicken in tip-top condition, you may encounter unusual ailments, deformities, or behavior issues in some of your birds. Though these oddities may be due to inbreeding, genetic abnormalities, or injury, you should act at the first sign that something is amiss. Immediately remove any birds that seem ill or have been injured. Treat these birds as quickly as possible. In some challenging cases, culling may present the best and most humane solution (The Happy Chicken Coop, 2015).

The Challenge With Harvesting

Butchering broilers for family meals in urban areas is unlikely to be your forte, nor will you have adequate specialized space to carry out the deed. If you've invested in broilers, you may need to negotiate with your local butchery to determine if they'll assist you with the harvesting process. If they agree, there may be a hefty cost involved.

Sometimes urbanites prefer doing the egg collecting thing, which is more accessible, less messy, and by far, the less stressful route to take (Whisperer, 2018).

You Aren't Alone

Rally the family, your friends, and neighbors to help with your chicken project. You never know when you may need a chicken sitter, so bring everyone on board from day one.

There will also likely be other backyard chicken keepers in your area that you can make contact with. Like you, these more experienced keepers may have helpful advice for when things get challenging. So, make contact and form a chicken-keeping network!

THE EFFECT OF CLIMATE ON YOUR BROOD'S PRODUCTIVITY

In the same way that hot, dry, or freezing weather affects you, your chickens are also susceptible to temperature changes. Unfortunately, your brood can't pull on an extra sweater or a pair of warm socks. It's up to you to provide for their needs. Should you fail to ensure their safety, security, warmth, and adequate ventilation, your chances of successfully raising backyard chickens are likely to diminish rapidly.

This book will show you some simple yet highly effective steps to overcome these challenges that will keep your chickens in peak condition, constantly happy, and productive (Liverpool-Tasie et al., 2019).

THE NEXT STEP

Now that you are genuinely excited about raising backyard chickens, let's get to the critical considerations required for preparing for the arrival of your quirky, loveable additions to the family.

2. THE IMPORTANCE OF PREPARATION

You're super excited by the prospect of being a backyard chicken keeper, but you may be asking yourself how to prepare for your chickens. Read on for lots of exciting and essential information to set you up for success.

Raising chickens requires a combination of basic knowledge, lots of enthusiasm, and careful preparation before jumping into the routine. Don't feel intimidated by the new hobby about which you may have little or no knowledge. As with most exciting and rewarding ventures like raising backyard chickens, preparation is the key to your success.

Once you've decided to embark on backyard chicken farming, you should look to start your chicken enterprise with day-old chicks, pullets, or by adopting an established flock. The fun in raising chicks from scratch (excuse the pun) is hard to beat. Though these tiny creatures require a great deal of constant care, they can start laying between 16 and 24 weeks. However, Smith (2020a) suggests it depends on the breed of chicken. The average hen can begin producing delicious eggs around eight months. The trick is not to lose hope. Each of your girls will lay when they're good and ready!

If you want to start with egg layers, invest in half a dozen pullets from a reputable supplier. These birds are on the point of laying, so they're ready to give you fresh eggs, and there will be no surprise roosters in the flock.

Taking on an established flock has some advantages. However, many of the birds may be approaching the end of their productive years. There may also e birds with illnesses or injuries that you may overlook while the flock is settling in.

Sometimes, chickens don't respond well to a change of environment. They also might be unsure about their new human caregivers and potentially afraid of any other pets you have. Any form of stress will negatively affect your new flock's productivity, so taking on an established flock of chickens can have drawbacks.

BRINGING YOUR FLOCK HOME

Taking care of your chicks is a reasonably straightforward exercise. All these little birds need is warmth, food, water, and maintenance. Loving your delightful chickens is the easiest thing in the world. What's not to love about these tiny balls of fluff? The chicks will respond positively to being handled with gentle care. As they grow up, the birds are likely to enjoy interaction with their human caregivers. The more endearing they become, the more you'll learn to love your feathered pets.

The brooder is your chickens' first home. Although there are plenty of ingenious ideas for brooders, a four-foot square, secure box with solid wood sides and a floor works best. The brooder should have a removable mesh lid for easy access for feeding and cleaning your new chicks. Positioned indoors, away from draughts and potential interference from noise and human or animal traffic, the brooder will be a haven for the day-old chicks.

Spread pine needles or good-quality straw on the floor of the box. Ensure your place a cozy, safe smaller basket or container in the brooder into which the chicks can snuggle. The tiny birds will also need water and grain in two separate, shallow containers.

Feeding your newbies with a good quality organic chick starter grain will ensure the chicks grow into healthy, productive hens.

To manage the brooder's hygiene, place a fine mesh grid on the straw and cover this with the sheet of a soft, absorbent, disposable towel. Scrape a small amount of chicken manure onto the sheet. It may take the chicks a little while to figure out that the towel is where they should poop, and once they have this under control, cleaning up after your little brood is that much easier.

Keep a close watch on your chicks, and if you notice any abnormalities, deformities, or feeding issues, a quick response is best. Check out reputable online sites for suggestions on how best to handle these health issues, or reach out to your local backyard chicken-raising community who are often your best allies.

THE SPACE CHALLENGE

Climate conditions, housing, feeding options, flock personalities, and different management techniques make it difficult to set the flock at a specified number. Although some chicken keepers specify detailed space per bird, a general rule is to keep your chicken community small and avoid trying to house too many birds in the available space.

Taking in more birds when space is restricted isn't in your flock's best interests. Overcrowding often leads to a wide variety of serious behavioral problems, including feather-pulling, bullying to outright fighting, and even cannibalism. Quite horrific, you'll agree (Ridgerunner, 2015)!

A crowded coop

There are many other issues to consider when planning space for your brood. To get started, you may want to consider using the FPSP program—flexibility, predators, security issues, and poop control.

Flexibility

Managing your brood in a relaxed and workable manner will ensure neither you nor your chickens suffer unnecessary stress. By sticking to set times, space, and feeding schedules, you may discover it's increasingly difficult to find someone to care for your yard chickens when you go away for a few days.

Predators

As has already been mentioned, because predators cause havoc among backyard chickens, it's essential to keep these unexpected critters under the best control you can manage. That said, your broods' safety takes precedence, which leads us to the next important point.

Security Issues

Invariably, a vital issue in the back of every chicken keeper's mind is the flock's safety. The coop and the fence around the run should be constructed of high-quality materials to ensure your brood's safety, security, ventilation, and warmth.

The larger the crowd of chickens, the more likely there will be fatalities from weaker birds being crushed or injured, as discussed above.

Poop Control

Whichever way you look at it, managing the poop load is crucial. The larger your poultry flock, the more significant the pile of manure! Since chickens poop during roosting and the birds aren't moving around, the poop piles up under the roosts.

Managing the poop load can be challenging, but after all, these delightful feathered friends rely solely on you for their health and welfare. So, it's off on poop clean up duty you go, morning and evening or whenever works best for you. The essential thing is not to leave the poop to build up, as the resulting health hazards will negatively impact the entire flock.

Positioning a removable dropping board or a mesh grid beneath the roosts can make the poop-cleaning process a great deal easier.

THE IDEAL CHICKEN COOP

All else considered, your chickens need a safe, secure enclosure with plenty of roosting areas and snug, dry nesting boxes. Housing requirements are one of the most critical aspects of successfully raising backyard chickens.

Generally, beginner chicken keepers prefer some basic guidelines to help them get started. A general rule of thumb for suburban chicken flocks is four square feet per chicken in the coop and eight to 10 square feet per bird in the run. Spacing is, however, flexible and dependent on the size of the coop, the run, and the breed.

If your flock is kept in a run daily, with space to move freely and adequate perching areas, there shouldn't be a problem. Remember, the coop is usually the part of the run, which gives those birds that prefer to be indoors the space to enjoy the nesting facilities.

You'll want the peace of mind that comes with knowing your feathered friends are safe and secure during the day and at night. They should have access to a secure coop situated at one end of the mesh-covered chicken run. The coop should be closed up for the night to avoid chickens being lost to wily, hungry predators.

There are many different types of coops on the market. Some are made from wood, while others are molded from toxic-free plastic. Though costly, you may prefer to buy a ready-made structure to save time.

If, however, you're handy with tools, you may want to build a henhouse. Use your imagination and initiative to create your chickens' very own, secure, cozy coop.

You'll find a few ideas in this chapter for suitable chicken coops for your precious flock.

LOCALE

Planning the location of your chicken coop and run is vital for the success of your venture. The law may stipulate how close the structure may be built to your home. However, consider your accessibility to the coop in all kinds of weather. The odor from the chickens' coop can sometimes be quite unpleasant, and the noise (hens can be incredibly noisy beasties!) will also play a role in your location choice.

Make use of a tree in your garden that may offer added protection and shade during the hotter months of the year. A variety of tasty grubs and edible crawlies live in trees and will supplement your chickens' meal plan rather nicely.

Bear in mind the weather and your flock's need for warmth during the colder months and shade in the hotter months. Installing windows on the south side of the coop if you live in the Northern Hemisphere or on the north-facing wall of the chicken coop if you're in the Southern Hemisphere will act as solar panels during the cold season.

Orient your coop's vents to ensure to get the best ventilation from the prevailing winds in your part of the world. However, the prevailing wind in your yard may be somewhat different, so consider this fact when erecting your coop. Remember, the chickens' coop needs adequate ventilation as well as insulation from dangerous, chilly draughts.

Placing the coop within a clear line of sight of your back porch or kitchen window will ensure you have your beady eye on the flock, and you won't miss the entertainment. Chickens also like to know their caregivers are close by and often come close to the fence to watch you. The birds will feel safer if you are within their line of sight, too.

A movable chicken house is becoming quite a popular choice because it's easy to reposition the structure to its best advantage throughout the year. Added to this, the lawn gets a much-needed chance to recuperate after having been decimated by scratching chickens!

CRITTER PROOFING

Protecting your chickens from would-be predators is one of the most significant challenges for all backyard chicken keepers.

Protect Openings

Chicken wire around the run is a fairly substantial measure to use against some predators. However, nothing much stops a hungry raccoon or hawk from feasting on members of your flock.

Ensure your birds are secure in the coop each evening. That way, they have the added protection of their sturdy, waterproof, weatherproof home. Early training your chickens to return to their pen at sunset will take the stress out of the birds being taken by nocturnal predators.

Use hardwire mesh to protect all openings in the coop. This rugged, sturdy product will help prevent weasels, snakes, and rodents from decimating your flock while you sleep. Hardwire mesh around the entire run will be a helpful though expensive option (Mormino, 2013).

Burrow Proofing

To keep burrowing predators out, you'll need to secure the floor of the coop. If the bottom of the run is attached to the walls, you may want to add hardwire mesh for added protection. In many cases, your best option is to carefully dig out the earth on which the run will stand, and lay chicken fencing covered with hardwire mesh into the area. Return the ground and stamp it down. Now, apply a concrete shoulder around the run's perimeter into which you place the metal or wooden stakes that will support the fence. Ensure the run walls are well-seated in the ground and build an apron to keep these in place (Mormino, 2013).

Secure the Run

Hard metal wire mesh makes a more secure cover for the chicken run. This product will give your flock added protection against flying predators during the day and at night.

Bolt the Doors

You may be starting to think you're building a goal. You aren't far wrong. When your flock is in the coop, you need to ensure all doors and windows are securely bolted. Some predators are clever enough to undo latches and hook-and-eye locks. Instead, consider using spring or barrel locks for added security (Mormino, 2013).

Eliminate Open Feeders

Grain placed in an open feeder attracts critters like rats and mice. Try the treadle feeder, which will eliminate this challenge. Your chickens are smart enough to learn to use this feed-on-demand device when they're hungry.

The suspended feeders are more successful because these can be hung higher than the average rodent can reach while still being accessible to your chickens.

Install Flock Guards

Roosters are great at setting off an early alarm. However, you may prefer not to keep one of these raucous birds, so instead, consider using geese or a suitable dog to guard the coop.

The Power of Deception

Erecting large decoy animals such as owls, alarms, bells, and motion sensor lights can keep predators at bay.

Mood Lighting

Ideal for stress-free chickens, mood lighting is an innovative energy-saving system that helps keep chickens calm during the night. By manipulating the light intensity in the coop and chicken run, the chickens find their way around better at night, and predators are less likely to want to investigate where there is light.

Lighting in the coop during the colder months also helps calm the hens and keep egg production consistent.

INDOORS/OUTDOORS

Do your chickens stay indoors or spend the day in the run? During bad weather, or when you're running late for work and don't have time to let your flock out of the coop, do the chickens have enough space to move around in the enclosure without turning into violent psychopaths? Once again, fewer birds will mean more freedom and less stress!

In colder climates, the coop can be made larger to accommodate the chickens that will spend much longer indoors than their counterparts that live in warmer areas. Consider about 10 square feet per bird if you live in these circumstances.

Should you decide on free-ranging your flock, you'll need to keep them secure in their coop for up to a week. This period will help to train the birds that the enclosure is their home and haven. After that, once you let the chickens roam freely, they'll come home to roost each evening at dusk, without fuss.

Personal Bird Space

Much like humans, your backyard chickens have different personalities. Some birds prefer their private space, while others you'll notice are more gregarious and love company. Larger birds require more space than smaller ones, while laying hens enjoy comfortably sized nesting boxes in a quieter area in the coop.

Observe your girls' individual needs and try as best you can to accommodate these. Happy chickens mean good egg production!

Adequate Roosting Space

Chickens enjoy roosting bars, which can be placed at varying heights in the run and the coop.

These bars effectively increase the area your flock can use and allow the birds the space to sit and preen in comfort or to roost in peace.

The chickens need enough space to fly to their roosting bars or hop onto these without knocking other birds. Chickens love to spread their wings, so there should be enough space for them to flap vigorously before settling in for the night.

Make sure your flock has adequate space to roost inside the coop at night. Ensure your chickens have enough perch space outside to enjoy whatever sun's rays might be available during the chilly winter days. Birds that roost close together during the cold winter nights will draw warmth from each other (DeannaCat, 2019).

SOME GREAT IDEAS
FOR YOUR COOP

DO CHICKENS HAVE MANNERS?

Though chickens are considered social birds, too much of a good thing can cause stress leading to fighting, aggressive behavior, a drop in egg laying, and even illness. By paying careful attention to your chickens' behavior, you can identify clues to what's going on in the flock that may help you prevent potential social disasters.

Dr. Jacob is a renowned chicken behaviorist at the University of Kentucky. Her insight into this intelligent, quirky birds' behavior has led to a deeper understanding of how chickens communicate and interact socially. She gives some great advice on certain behaviors for which beginner chicken keepers can look out (Jacob, n.d.).

HEN AND CHICK BEHAVIOR

Most hens take good care of their eggs. They brood for about three weeks, regularly turning their eggs during this period to ensure the even distribution of warmth and moisture over the entire egg.

A mother hen vocalizes while she's brooding, and it's believed the chicks recognize her "voice" the minute they hatch out of their eggs. The high-pitched "piping" that chicks make starts while they're in their final incubation stages in the egg. These sounds alert their mother to their imminent arrival.

Once the chicks hatch, the mother hen is usually profoundly focused on her chicks and takes care of them for up to about two months. They form a tight-knit little family, which allows the chicks to mimic their mother as she scratches and feeds. There's a great deal of vocalizing during this time, and one must assume these sounds are part of the family discussion time. The chicks also identify their mother's call from among all the other hens in the coop.

The mother hen will teach her chicks to drink water. Without a hen to mimic, chicks can die of thirst even if they're standing in water. Their instinct to drink is stimulated by seeing bubbles or tiny grains in the water or copying their mother hen's actions. Once the chicks peck at the water in response to the visual stimulus, their drinking reflex is encouraged.

The hens appear not to show favoritism to their chicks. It's very much a case of first come, first served, so the more robust chicks always take precedence.

A mother hen will usually protect her chicks until her final breath. She also offers these tiny balls of fluff, solace, shade, and security by tucking her little ones under her wings (Jacob, n.d.).

CHICK TO CHICK BEHAVIOR

During the first three days after hatching, chicks usually stick close together, gaining warmth and comfort from each other. Sadly, however, the laws of nature will always prevail. After about 15 to 16 days, fights for dominance may break out. Among groups of female chicks, the pecking order is quickly resolved. However, male chicks can continue their aggressive behavior for months.

Survival of the fittest and biggest remains the single most crucial factor. A definite "pecking order" develops early. The more robust chicks generally lead the way, closely following their mother's example for scratching, feeding, drinking, and preening. The leader chicks respond sooner to changes in the environment. For example, when a heater is turned on, more alert chicks will be the first to move toward the heat source. In some instances, weaker chicks are discarded or sometimes pecked to death by their siblings (Jacob, n.d.).

Keep a watchful eye over your day-olds to ensure each of the chicks has a fair chance at survival.

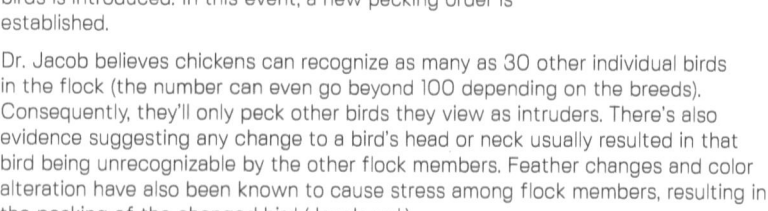

ADULT BIRD BEHAVIOR

Adult chickens have developed the ability to recognize members of their flock. The pecking order is strictly adhered to unless a larger group of new birds is introduced. In this event, a new pecking order is established.

Dr. Jacob believes chickens can recognize as many as 30 other individual birds in the flock (the number can even go beyond 100 depending on the breeds). Consequently, they'll only peck other birds they view as intruders. There's also evidence suggesting any change to a bird's head or neck usually resulted in that bird being unrecognizable by the other flock members. Feather changes and color alteration have also been known to cause stress among flock members, resulting in the pecking of the changed bird (Jacob, n.d.).

Preening

Feathers are composed of a central shaft from which long, delicate structures protrude. These delicate parts of the feather hook onto each other to create a waterproof shield. Sometimes, the hooks or barbs become separated. The chickens use their beaks to collect a small amount of oil from their preen gland, situated at their tail base. They then run their beaks over those feathers that need to be realigned. This process is called preening. Tip-top feather maintenance is crucial for waterproofing and insulation (Jacob, n.d.).

Fighting

Unfortunately, fighting is part and parcel of the chicken's life. From an early age, these once dear fluffy harmless-looking little birds become aggressive warriors who fight to set up the pecking order, win a mate, and sometimes even to challenge a dominant bird's position.

Fights begin with two birds circling and eyeing each other attentively. The birds then fluff their neck feathers, drop their wings down, and stretch their bodies as tall as possible. This change in stature creates the illusion of each being bigger and more menacing than they were before. If neither bird backs down, the chickens will jump and flap at each other, pecking and scratching until one bird dominates the other. On rare occasions, these fights can end in severe injury to the birds and even death (Jacob, n.d.).

Foraging

In their search for food, chickens use their age-old foraging technique to scratch up unsuspecting critters hiding in the grass or beneath small stones. Although your backyard chickens are probably well-fed, their instinctive behavior to forage is part of what makes these creatures so exciting and worthy of the title bug annihilators (Jacob, n.d.).

Nesting

Much like you enjoy snuggling under your cozy duvet, your backyard chickens will love nesting in loose, dry material like straw or pine needles. They shuffle and wriggle to mold the nesting material around their bodies and feet snuggly. Pullets that fail to learn to nest correctly will likely lay their eggs on the coop floor instead of in a nesting box. In these cases, you can place an artificial egg into the nesting box to encourage your reluctant pullet to brood in the box.

Pre-laying behavior begins when the chicken starts poking around the nesting boxes. The bird may become restless and a little fussy until she selects a specific nesting box into which she will finally settle.

Once the pullet lays the egg, she may cackle and flap her wings a little to announce her success before leaving the nest to continue her daily activities. If, for some reason, the hen is disturbed or becomes stressed during her egg-laying procedure, she may drop her egg elsewhere in the run or on the range. Worse than this, she may retain the egg, leading to severe health problems for the hen (Jacob, n.d.). Read more about this in chapter four.

Dust Bathing

Unpleasant as this behavior may sound to a beginner chicken keeper, it plays an essential role in your chickens' lifestyle and grooming. Rolling in dust helps rid the chickens of mites, dry skin, and other irritations. The process also reduces oil buildup on the feathers. Fortunately, you can enjoy a shower instead of dust bathing!

Perching

One thing chickens love to do is perching. At about three weeks old, these little birds begin to practice jumping onto higher structures where they use their cleverly designed claws to cling to these perches tightly.

For most birds, perching affords them the chance to view their world from a higher vantage point. This activity also allows the chickens to use elevated space instead of always being at ground level.

Perching space is essential in every coop and chicken run as it increases the available space for the birds to use to not only change positions but also find a private spot to preen or rest.

About an hour before sunset, your birds will begin to go into the coop to roost. The majority of your chickens spend their sleeping hours huddled together in small groups, perching on their roosting struts, until just before dawn.

Response to Ambient Temperature

The ambient temperature is the level of heat or cold around an object, which, in this case, is your chicken. As a rule, chickens prefer cooler conditions. Your flock is highly susceptible to overheating. Signs of their increasing discomfort may include head dunking into the water, excessive flapping, and sometimes panting. Be alert to these signs and respond immediately to avoid heat stress.

Opening vents in the coop or using a fan to circulate the air will stabilize the ambient temperature on hot days.

Drinking

Water is an essential life-giving resource which your chickens also need to soften the grain they eat. Insufficient water intake may result in grain-clumping in the chicken's crop. These lumps of grain harden and exert pressure on the chicken's carotid artery, which may hinder blood flow to the brain. The effects of this lack of oxygen can lead to seizures, paralysis, and even death. Always ensure your flock has plenty of clean fresh water (Jacob, n.d.).

FEATURES BEGINNERS LOOK FOR

Though some breeds are more attractive-looking than others, your choice of a suitable breed is dependent on more than just appearance. To get the best out of your flock, consider the following aspects.

- General temperament and disposition
- Hardiness to temperature fluctuations
- Egg-laying ability and meat suitability

There are a wide variety of breeds from which to choose your starting flock. However, because the choice is so vast, below are several suggestions among which you are bound to find a breed or two that will best suit your needs and climate (Smith, 2020).

SUITABLE BREEDS FOR BEGINNERS

As a beginner backyard chicken keeper, you'll probably be wondering which breeds to choose, what characteristics to look for, and where to source your stock.

Wherever you decide to get your chicks, always make sure the supplier is reputable. Chicks can be sourced from online or local hatcheries or farm stores. In some cases, chicks are also available from particular hardware stores.

Most hatcheries sell "sexed" chicks, which means those you buy are hens. If you purchase "straight-run" chicks from a farm or hardware store, there is likely to be a surprise rooster or two among the flock of hens.

As with all livestock purchases, you should consider minimizing the challenges to yourself and your chicks.

Chicks that are shipped often arrive stressed and may not all be in the best of health. Fatalities can occur during the trip due to delays or changes in weather conditions. The birds may also take time to acclimatize, which could potentially lead to more health issues.

Purchasing your chicks from a reputable local hatchery is less likely to be as traumatizing. There is often a better selection, and the chicks are far more likely to adapt to their new home quickly. You also don't have the stress of waiting for your precious brood to arrive, and there's no hassle with shipping costs.

BUFF ORPINGTON

The Buff Orpington chickens are a great favorite. Light brown, these dual-purpose chickens are raised for eggs and meat. This delightful, sweet-natured breed of chickens is

usually calm and docile. These birds lay not only copious numbers of eggs but also make great pets.

CINNAMON QUEEN

This modern high-yielding variety is a Rhode Island Red/White hybrid with glossy brown feathers. These easy-to-tame, highly attentive birds make an attractive addition to your flock. The Cinnamon Queen is a prolific egg layer and ideal for beginner backyard chicken keepers.

DOMINIQUE

Considered the oldest breed dating back to colonial days, the Dominique (Pilgrim Fowl) is a magnificent, stylish bird with attractive barred plumage. Similar in color to their Plymouth Rock cousins, Dominique hens have a flatter comb.

Perfect for beginner chicken keepers, these birds are easy to rear and have a gentle, calm temperament unless they feel threatened. Dominique chickens are good "gardeners," foraging for bugs and turning the soil. They're often broody and make excellent mothers. You can expect up to four eggs per week from each hen (Lesley, 2020c).

EASTER EGGER

Now, here's another fascinating hybrid with the blue egg gene.

Depending on the gene they carry, Easter Eggers lay eggs with blue to varying shades of brown. Each hen lays a large number of specific colored eggs during its lifetime. Sweet-natured and attractive, these delightful birds make a great addition to your flock.

HYBRID—SPECKLEDY HENS

This elegant, attractive hybrid with its gorgeous, soft, silky, speckled plumage closely resembles a Marans hen. Speckledy hens have pale eyes and legs and smaller earlobes and wattles.

Their gentle, sweet, chatty, easy-to-tame nature makes them a popular choice for beginning backyard chicken farmers. Speckledy hens can lay as

many as 270 speckled brown eggs per year and make a welcome addition to your flock.

LEGHORN

The Leghorn is a famous, easy-to-breed chicken that's active and constantly foraging. These birds are hardy and less susceptible to illnesses and setbacks than some other breeds. Leghorns are excellent egg layers that can produce as many as 300 in one year. These chickens are a perfect choice for beginner chicken keepers.

PLYMOUTH ROCK

Perhaps the most popular breed in the United States, these attractive, hardy birds have mainly a black and white striped plumage. Plymouth Rock chickens are a gentle, docile, dual-purpose breed that produces magnificent brown eggs. These birds will make a colorful addition to your flock.

RHODE ISLAND REDS

These majestic, attractive chickens are an excellent choice for any beginner chicken keeper. They're remarkably low in maintenance, hardy, dual-purpose chickens that lay between five and seven eggs a week. They're suitable for a variety of climates, though they do best in less favorable conditions. Rhode Island Red chickens are a worthwhile investment for beginner chicken keepers.

If you have not yet, feel free to download the Chicken Breeds Selection Helper at the beginning of the book to assist you in your choice.

THE NEXT STEP

Now that you've learned the importance of preparing for your flock, choosing the best chicken run and coop, as well as the breeds that will suit your needs and the climate, you're ready for the next step.

Let's take a look at the importance of feeding your flock correctly to ensure the chickens' optimum health and egg production.

3 HEALTHY FEEDING HABITS

Now that you have a good idea of the breed of chickens you'd like to invest in, and you've got the chicken house all sorted, what about the flock's feeding requirements? In this chapter, you'll find plenty of information about the best feed for your cute chickens, as well as tips on which foods to avoid. There are ideas for tasty snacks that range from table scraps to the importance of organic feeds.

Science has taught us that a well-balanced diet with plenty of fresh air, regular exercise, and a good sleep routine is ideal for keeping our bodies in tip-top condition. Believe it or not, the same is true for your feathered family.

Chicken feed has developed into a surprisingly complex science involving extensive research and a great deal of thought and planning. Gone are the days when a handful of grain tossed to homegrown hens sufficed their feed needs. Commercially manufactured poultry feed contains balanced nutrients, which will afford your chickens the best chance of growth and egg production.

WHAT CHICKENS EAT

Chickens eat a surprising selection of foods that will keep them in peak health. This chapter deals with how to develop healthy eating habits for your chooks. Gosh, and you thought it was only you who had to watch their diet!

Chickens are omnivores. That means, like you, they eat vegetables, fruits, carbohydrates, and proteins. When ranging in your yard, you'll be surprised by the number of bugs and critters your beady-eyed flock finds apart from tasty clover, seeds, and other nutritious foods.

Instinctively, your chickens know they need to eat a variety of foods. Apart from vegetation, fruits, and grass seeds, chickens will basically taste just about anything that moves, sometimes to their detriment. It appears this is the only way they can figure out what's good to eat and what's best left alone. Lizards, toads, skinks, and even a tiny snake may end up being tossed aside as your girls decide on their best dietary needs.

As already mentioned, fresh food and water are a daily necessity for all pets and livestock. Layer feed is the best for your poultry. Filled with the correct balance of nutrients for laying hens, this feed type should be of good quality and bought from a reputable supplier so that you know there are no dangerous additives included (Telkamp, 2019).

You can order suitable feed from online suppliers, hatcheries, retailers, and many stores that sell farm supplies. Many suppliers offer advice about ideal grain feeds, and they may also sell the necessary equipment for feeding and watering your chickens. However, beware of buying from a catalog unless you're sure the product is suitable for your flock's needs.

Where possible, feed your chickens organically. There are several reputable suppliers of organic poultry feeds. You may be able to buy some of these from your local town store. The critical thing to remember is that suppliers closer to you are preferable as running out of grain can have disastrous results (Purina, 2019).

During the summer, while your chickens are on the range, feeding is just that much easier. Besides bugs and some grain, your flock will probably enjoy clover, Kentucky bluegrass, and buckwheat. However, extra dietary supplements are likely necessary during the cold months, as successful foraging will be minimal at this time (Telkamp, 2019).

WATER MANAGEMENT
Like you, your chickens will undoubtedly survive longer without food than without water. However, your flock needs both to reach their optimum growth and development.

A lack of constant fresh water will cause growth delays, early molting, stress, and it will also alter the egg-laying patterns in your flock.

Apart from automatic watering units, which can be a costly investment, a water fountain can make a fun place for your birds to drink while they enjoy the spray to cool themselves off on hot summer days.

FEED MANAGEMENT
As mentioned, your chickens need to eat and drink daily. Not only is food essential for the growth and development of your chickens, but it also generates heat to maintain their body temperature and helps in the production of delicious eggs (Linden, 2015).

Clever management of the food and water containers can add space and interest to the chicken run. Use your ingenuity to find a suitable way of managing the containers to avoid the contents being soiled. Securing these repositories above ground level will afford the birds an added perching area less likely to become contaminated by their poop than when containers are on the chicken run floor.

Some backyard chicken keepers have dishes enclosed by rigid wire mesh attached to one outside coop wall. Small slots above each container, suitably sized to allow the chickens to poke their heads through, will enable the chickens' access to food and water without the challenge of poop contamination. The containers are easy to fill with grain and water without opening the coop, which helps when the weather gets nasty.

TYPES OF CHICKEN FEED

Wheat

Durum wheat is the best and most nutritious grain for poultry feeds. It should be fed in course scratch feeds or mashes. Wheat forms the basis for most poultry feed to which a variety of other grains are added.

Oats

This grain can be added as whole hulls, rolled, or as a mash. The nutrient value of oats depends on the hull content.

Barley

This grain is a valuable additive as a whole grain to scratch feeds. It can also be rolled or mashed. Soaked or boiled barley also works well.

Corn

Chickens love corn and will eat it whole, cracked, or crushed. It can be served alone or with other grains.

Millet

Proso, or hog millet, is fantastic for growing, fattening, and laying. It is often used as the two-thirds component in many feeds.

Rye

Though not as palatable as the other grains, small rye quantities can be added to both scratch and mash feeds.

Flax

This grain is ideal for adding to scratch feed in the molting season and during fall and winter.

Grain By-Products

Bran, shorts, and middlings are great to add to growing and laying rations.

Oat flour, feed, middlings, and barley flour are added to fattening rations.

Fats

Most feeds contain a small quantity of fat needed as an energy source and help the chicken's body absorb essential vitamins. Besides excess fat being dangerous to your health, it can cause severe digestive problems for your chickens.

Animal and vegetable fats are a high source of energy. They improve the absorption of minerals and vitamins and support improved digestion. Introducing a small amount of fat into your chickens' diet can be beneficial.

Milk By-Products

All milk by-products help laying hens and fatten birds, as well as support high-quality hatching. These components are considered vital additives for high-quality poultry feeds.

Fish Oil

Many types of fish oil

supplements are added to chick rations, winter feeds, and feeds for laying hens, especially when their vegetable rations are in short supply.

Balancers

Fillers and balancers are specially prepared food supplements made by poultry feed manufacturers and should be added to traditional poultry feed according to the manufacturer's instructions (Manitoba, 1945).

CHOOSING THE PERFECT FEED FOR YOUR FLOCK

The type of feed you choose for your backyard flock depends rather heavily on what your plans are for your birds. Broilers are treated differently from egg-laying chickens, so be sure you know which type of birds you have before you plan for their specific dietary needs.

Chick Feed

Feed for chicks is divided into starter (20-24% protein) and growing feed (18% protein). From hatching to about six weeks of age, starter feed is perfect for your new little birds. When your chicks reach six to seven weeks of age, gradually change them to growing mash, rich in crucial nutrients for your chicks' continued growth and development.

Layers

Organic, non-GMO (Genetically Modified Organism) layer feed, rich in essential nutrients and with about 16% protein, is the ideal choice for pullets that are starting to lay. There's a wide variety of suitable commercial feeds on the market from which to choose. These pullets will remain on this feed for the majority of their lives.

Broilers/Meat Birds

If you decide to raise meat birds, you'll need to supply these chickens with feed with a higher percentage of protein (around 22%) than what layers require. Because the turnaround time for broilers is faster than layers, broilers need feed that will help them grow faster and fatten sooner than their egg-laying cousins.

A broiler's lifespan is about 14 weeks. Within that short time, these birds need to be sufficiently fattened for culling.

All Flock Feeds

Most backyard chicken keepers have birds of varying ages in their flock. All Flock Feed is perfect for these birds' needs. Most of these balanced feeds have added probiotics that aid digestion and support good gut health.

All Flock Feed makes a great maintenance feed for adult birds.

Fermented Feed

Many backyard chicken keepers mix feed with water. Believe it or not, fermented feed is not only healthier for your chickens but also less costly in the long run. Fermenting is quick and easy to do.

To any grain you currently feed your chickens, add a little water and a few drops of apple cider vinegar. Mix together in a suitable nontoxic plastic container. Add teaspoon yeast and stir in well.

Allow the container to stand for three to four days, by which time the mixture should smell like sourdough. The fermented feed is ready to be fed to your chickens that will undoubtedly enjoy this delicious treat.

The gourmet menu available for your chickens includes a wide variety of delectable delights. Among these feed options, you are likely to find the following:

Pellets
This poultry feed is sustainable, low-wastage adult chicken feed that has been formed into easy-to-store methods, transportable, and use pellet form.

Crumbles
One size down from pellets are crumbles which consist of crushed pellets suitable for chicks.

Mash
The finely crushed, assorted, unprocessed feed that comes in powder form is called mash. Suitable for day-old chicks as well as adult birds, the mash can be served wet or dry. As with all feed, adequate fresh water is an essential element for chickens to digest their dinner properly.

Fermented Feed
When regular chicken feed is mixed with water and allowed to ferment naturally, the chickens are likely to benefit from the delicious nutrients released during this process.

Medicated Feed
Some poultry feeds are treated with a coccidiostat, a preventative substance that supports improved gut health in kittens, puppies, cattle, and poultry and delays the growth and reproduction of the deadly parasitic *Coccidian protozoa*.

Unmedicated Feed
All regular untreated poultry feed without added coccidiostat falls into the category of unmedicated feed.

FEED INGREDIENTS

For healthy development, chickens need a diet rich in protein, fats, minerals, carbohydrates, and vitamins. Sound familiar? Your dietary needs include the same essential macro and micronutrients. Let's take a more detailed look at each of these nutritional components.

Macronutrients
These nutrients are essential for the optimum health, well-being, and productivity of your backyard flock and include proteins, carbohydrates, and fats.

Proteins
Often referred to as the body's building blocks, proteins are not only a vital energy source, but they also help to build and repair damaged tissues and cells.

Often the most expensive poultry feed component, protein sources include meat, fish scraps, milk, nuts, and bone meal. A well-balanced feed of grain and assorted protein is your best choice for raising a thriving, healthy poultry flock.

Carbohydrates
These essential components consist of the starchy ingredients in the feed that support energy release. Carbohydrates make up the most significant percentage of your chickens' dietary needs. They are vital for energy and optimum body function. Though crucial in your chickens' diet, as previously mentioned, chickens can't survive adequately on carbohydrates alone.

Fats
For the optimum health of your backyard flock, the general rule is to exclude fatty foods from their diet.

Micronutrients
Just as essential and vital for chicken health are the following

micronutrients, which include vitamins, minerals, and riboflavin.

Vitamin A

Micronutrients like vitamins are essential for the growth, health, and longevity of your flock. When your chickens don't enjoy a balanced diet, certain problems may arise.

Your chickens may develop a susceptibility to infections and colds as a result of a vitamin A deficiency. Increase their greens, corn, and fish oil intake.

Vitamin D

If your flock shows signs of leg weakness, bone deformities, and soft eggshells, this may result from vitamin D deficiency. Increase the fish oil content in the chicken feed and encourage your flock to enjoy more time in the sunshine.

Riboflavin

This vitamin, found in yeast, green feed, liver, and milk products, is essential for the growth and development of chicks in the shell until they reach adults. If your flock exhibits curled toe paralysis, a riboflavin deficiency may be the reason.

Minerals

Essential minerals include calcium, magnesium, manganese, phosphorus, potassium, and zinc, all of which play a vital role in bone strength and structure, tendon strength and flexibility, and eggshell manufacture. Salt and specific green feeds are rich in these micronutrients.

THE BEST WAYS TO FEED YOUR FLOCK

Although you may believe you can prepare a balanced diet for your chooks, as a beginner keeper, it might be easier and simpler to buy a commercially prepared starter and growing mash because essential components have already been added to these feeds.

Young chicks require a carefully balanced diet rich in vitamins, proteins, and minerals. Two pounds of dry starter mash will usually feed one chick for six weeks. After that, unless your chicks are broilers, slowly introduce coarser grains until the young pullets are on the same diet as the flock adults. Broilers should stay on a more concentrated diet to fatten quickly. Though it can be pretty expensive, a commercially produced starter feed is often the easiest route. Choose a flaky or mealy variety to avoid the feed clumping in the chickens' mouths and causing unwanted, potentially expensive digestive problems for your flock.

STARTER FEEDS

Start feeding chicks as soon as they show an interest in eating. Place shallow containers or use egg case flats in several spots around the run. Ensure every chick has learned to eat. Some chicks get the idea right from the start, while others are slower to realize they should be pecking at the food. If you notice a slow starter, you'll have to intervene to help the weaker chick figure out the eating process.

FEEDING THE CORRECT RATIONS

Linden (2015) reminds us that commercial feed contains a great variety of healthy ingredients. However, the type of rations you choose will depend on a number of important factors, including:

1. The age of your flock
2. The breed
3. Whether your birds are laying hens or broiler

FEEDS IDEAL FOR GROWING AND DEVELOPING

By weeks six and seven, your chicks should be on a fifty-fifty mix of starter and growing mash. After that, the chicks can use whole grain self-feeders, or you may find suspended plastic dishes at a suitable height for the pullets serve the purpose just the same.

Place small trays of fine grit in hoppers separate from the food. Add a little cracked wheat to the feed at three weeks and whole wheat at four weeks (Manitoba, 1945).

A good supply of milk to drink will help these chicks absorb the calcium their tiny bones need. However, if the pullets show signs of growing too quickly, reduce their milk intake.

Ensure your chicks have an adequate supply of clean, fresh, and aerated water. The bubbles in the water encourage the chicks to drink.

Make an excellent effort to supply your flock with good-quality green pasture for as many months as possible. Fall rye, oats, and alfalfa provide a nutritious range for newly hatched chicks. Add crushed corn to their diet for added carbohydrate bulk.

If your environment permits, good healthy pasture feeding lowers the cost of commercial feeds and encourages strong bone growth and glossy feather development.

LAYING RATIONS

For egg-laying hens to be fully productive and bring you great satisfaction, these birds should be fed laying rations for most of the year, to which extra protein supplements have been added. Because profit depends on eggs' steady production, it's essential to ensure your flock also has adequate vitamins and minerals added to their diet. Increase the uptake of alfalfa, clover hay, coarse grains, and skim milk to ensure your hens produce the best eggs.

During the winter months, your hens may not drink enough milk and take insufficient protein and minerals. Thus, it's essential to supplement their feed with commercial fillers, balancers, laying concentrates, and various protein meal types.

Crushed oyster shells, limestone grit, and bone meal are essential additions to your flock's dietary needs.

TABLE SCRAPS

Because table scraps are not part of your flock's regular diet, feeding these in moderation is advisable. Chickens are notoriously hungry and will often eat just about anything. Take great care to choose suitable scraps and only start feeding these to your flock once the birds are between three and four months old. Chicks are still growing; therefore, they shouldn't be fed scraps but instead encouraged to eat the growing mash (McMurray Staff, 2017).

Suitable Scraps
Certain scraps to incorporate in the chickens' diet include (McMurray Staff, 2017):

- Limited quantities of bread that isn't moldy
- Cooked meats cut into small pieces
- Raw, cooked, or dried corn
- Fruits including grapes, apples, watermelon, and berries
- Grains including rice, wheat, and commercial cereals
- Raw or cooked vegetables including peas, broccoli, shredded carrots, cabbage, spinach, potatoes, squash, lettuce, tomatoes, kale, yogurt, and pasta

Scraps to Avoid
On the contrary, the scraps that should be avoided include (McMurray Staff, 2017):

- Salt
- Processed meats
- Takeout foods and pastries
- Raw potato skins
- Avocado peels and pits
- Spoiled foods
- Coffee, tea, and soft drinks
- Chocolate
- Greasy foods
- Garlic
- Onions
- Chili peppers
- Raw meat

ORGANIC FEEDS
If eating organic is a healthier solution for you, it'll work exceptionally well for your flock. Organic chicken feed is likely to have similar health and long-term benefits for your backyard chickens.

Organic foods are farmed in a healthy, natural, and sustainable way without pesticides or any damaging practices that may reduce the quality and food value of the end product. Baby chick crumbs and mixed corn are just two organic products you may find helpful.

The Benefits of Organic Chicken Feeds Land (Farm & Pet Place, 2016):
- No toxic additives to the soil
- Well-managed, sustainable land management
- No contamination of natural water sources
- No damage to the natural landscape
- No harm to animal wildlife
- No pollutants or GM food production

Poultry (Farm & Pet Place, 2016):
- More nutritious feed
- No GMO in food
- Few toxins in soil and water
- You're bringing nutritious, organic meat and eggs to your table.

Suppliers of Organic Feeds (Farm & Pet Place, 2016):
Among the best organic brands are Marriages, Purina, and Allen & Page.

EMERGENCY FEED
Sometimes things go awry, and life throws you the proverbial "curveball." You may find yourself in the uncompromising situation of having run out of chicken feed. Well, apart from feeling bad about your lack of planning and before your flock withdraws into sulk mode, here's some quick, easy advice to calm

ruffled feathers and give yourself time to restock the chicken's larder (Arcuri L., 2012):

1. Hard-boiled eggs, cooled and chopped, make a delicious treat for your hungry brood.
2. Good old table scraps will suffice for a day or two.
3. Hand-plucked suitable grasses and clovers will keep the flock happy.
4. Porridge is an excellent standby in emergencies.

YUMMY SNACKS

Most people enjoy treats and snacks, especially when these aren't always the healthiest foods on the menu. Think chocolate, candy bars, popcorn, and ice cream cones!

Chickens love snacks, too. The only significant difference here is that their treats should be healthy. Don't tell your girls there isn't a chocolate sundae on their menu!

Here are some great ideas for chicken treats that will have your birds worshipping the ground you tread on, albeit just for the goodies!

Mealworms are sure to be a massive favorite among your flock. Add blackberries, blueberries, grated carrot, and sunflower seeds to the mix, and you'll have hit the jackpot with your girls.

Just remember, no matter how much begging, pushing, shoving, and cajoling your girls do, snacks are treats that shouldn't be shelled out willy-nilly. Instead, these tasty tidbits should be given at specific times, such as early morning before you leave for work or when you're training your flock to go into the coop at night. It's up to you to decide how best to manage the treats to avoid a snack attack!

However, if you follow the 90/10 feeding rule, your chickens will remain healthy and productive without gaining extra unnecessary weight.

See more ideas in the "Fun and Games" section in chapter seven.

THE 90/10 FEEDING RULE

This advice is fundamental for the maintenance of the optimum health and productivity of your flock. In other words, 90% of the chickens' food should consist of nutritious, well-balanced feed. The remaining 10% can be made up of snacks, treats scraps, and scratch grain (Jim, 2020).

FEEDING MISTAKES TO AVOID

According to Linden (2015), the greatest challenge is to choose the correct feed for your chooks to keep the birds in peak condition. Without being aware of these potentially harmful errors, you could inadvertently be starving your flock of essential nutrients. The results may be inadequate egg production and chickens that quickly fall prey to disease.

Error Number One

Avoid giving your young birds a layer feed, as the calcium levels are too high. Don't mix scratch grain such as cracked corn with commercial feeds as this reduces the protein, vitamin, and mineral content of the feed.

Table 1 lists the correct rations that should be fed and the percentages for each.

Error Number Two

According to Linden (2015), the second mistake is not feeding your chickens enough of the appropriate food choice.

Table 2 lists an estimate of feed consumption and the kinds of feed required by healthy chickens.

Table 1

Type/Age	Protein %	Calcium %	Fiber %	Fats %	Phosphorus %
Broilers					
Starter 1-3 weeks	22	0.9	2.5	6.0	0.6
Finisher 4-7 weeks	19	0.8	2.5	7.0	0.5
Pullets					
Starter 1-6 weeks	20	0.9	3.0	4.0	0.5
Grower 7-8 weeks	17	0.8	4.0	3.5	0.5
Laying Hens 19 weeks+	16-18	3.3-4.0	3.5	3.5	0.5

Table 2

Type/Age	Total of Feed (lbs)	Ration
Layers (Brown egg)		
Day-old to 6 weeks	4	Starter
7-18 weeks	46	Grower
19-70 weeks	104	Layer
Layer (White egg)		
Day-old to 6 weeks	3	Starter
7-18 weeks	12	Grower
19-70 weeks	80	Layer
Broilers (Meat)		
Day-old to 3 weeks	2	Starter
4-7 weeks	7	Finisher

Due to the fact that more than 70% of the cost of raising your brood is feed, this is an investment. The better nourished your chickens, the more likely they'll remain healthy and productive for their life span (Linden, 2015).

THE NEXT STEP

Although taking good care of your flock takes effort and a keen sense of duty, good food, good water management, and sound knowledge of the suitable feed for your chooks will go a long way to ensure your feathered family's health and success.

Closely related to feeding is the health and fitness of the flock. Let's dive into the importance of keeping your chickens on their toes.

4 YOUR BROOD'S HEALTH AND FITNESS

What if your chickens fall ill, get injured, or suffer from a disease? How will you care for these new members of your pet family?

As a backyard chicken keeper, you'll want to ensure your flock stays in peak health for the duration of their life and thus avoids harmful health issues.

Now that your backyard flock is established and laying, you're well on the road to successful chicken keeping. Make sure to supply your birds with clean, fresh water and food daily. Keep the coop clean and dry. Collect your eggs regularly and keep an eye on your flock for changes in behavior or eating habits that may signal disease or injuries.

Unless you're particularly observant, you may fail to notice these changes in your chickens as the birds can be highly adept at hiding their distress. Watch for pullets that appear miserable, quiet, withdrawn, or overly anxious and aggressive. Chickens that are ill may often lose feathers and become listless.

However, despite your best efforts, several factors can weaken your chickens, and sadly, in some cases, lead to the death of some of your treasured birds.

Bentoli (2017) nutritional experts suggest in addition to a hygienic, well-managed flock, optimal nutrient intake is an essential ingredient for your flock's health and well-being. Added to their quality feed, approved supplements and additives effectively boost the poultry's immune system and support your chickens' healthy growth and development.

COMMON HEALTH PROBLEMS AMONG YOUR CHICKENS

It's vitally important to be aware of the common health problems your poultry may face and learn to recognize and treat these as soon as you become aware of them. One of the challenging aspects of chicken keeping is that your dear birds are natural prey animals with a highly intuitive way of managing their pain and discomfort. It's therefore difficult to know if one of the flock members is ill.

Expect your backyard chickens to lay eggs well for the first two years before beginning to dwindle. The decision to remove those chickens that have stopped laying eggs can be fraught with misery, especially if the hens have been treated as pets, and culling is the only answer.

Many chicken keepers simply allow the older hens to live out the remainder of their lives in peace as a gesture of gratitude for the eggs received.

Though some health problems are difficult to detect, while others can decimate your flock within hours, being on the lookout for potential issues will be in your flock's best interests. So, what's wrong with your chicken? How can you help? Here are just six of the most common illnesses that can have devastating effects on backyard chickens and their keepers.

EGG-LAYING PROBLEMS

Once your backyard flock has been established, it won't be long before you're rewarded with freshly laid eggs. The laying cycle is dependent on the breed, the season, and how happy and content your chickens are.

It's crucial to set up good training for your flock to lay eggs in the specially provided nesting boxes. Range hens don't know these boxes. As soon as your backyard flock members develop brighter combs, it's often a sign they're ready to lay. Lesley (2020) suggests placing "dummy eggs" in several nesting boxes to encourage the hens to lay eggs in these receptacles. Lock these ready to lay chickens up for about a week so that they learn to lay without interruption.

Formation of the Egg

The egg is formed in the chicken's ovary from where it moves down the oviduct, gathering yolk, albumin, membranes, and finally, its shell. Once the process is complete, the egg is ready to be laid. Amazingly, depending on the breed of hen, some chickens can lay as many as six eggs per week.

The egg exits the hen's body through the vent, which is the same opening through which feces and urine are expelled. Nature has a miraculous way of allowing the chicken to lay eggs without pooping all over them. A short distance from the vent is an intersection in the hen's body where the digestive and urinary tracts meet. This opening is called the cloaca. The cloaca usually closes when the hen lays an egg.

Egg Discrepancies

Egg-laying discrepancies are one of the first clues that something is wrong with one of your hens. Acute symptoms that can give you a clue that all is not well in your flock may include:

- A sudden change of behavior in one hen
- Loss of appetite
- Weakness
- Respiratory issues
- Abnormal droppings
- The hen's inability to lay eggs or laying abnormal eggs

As a rule, most chickens have little or no difficulties laying normal-shaped eggs. However, there may be odd occasions when there's an abnormality. Don't panic! Let's look at some of the potential causes of abnormal egg laying and how best to resolve these challenges.

EGG YOLK PERITONITIS

This abnormality occurs when the egg yolk develops in the chicken's abdominal cavity, causing an inflammatory response. If left untreated, this situation can lead to the chicken's death.

Symptoms:
You'll know when your hens aren't well, as although they can't speak, their body language says it all—lack of appetite, lethargy, respiratory distress, yellow-colored poop, and dropping feathers.

Treatment:
Antibiotics and hormones are often the best solutions. Your veterinarian will advise you of the route to use.

LASH EGGS

Lash eggs, also known as salpingitis, result from inflammation in the oviduct caused by E. Coli or Mycoplasma. High production and older birds are often the most affected by lash egg syndrome.

Lesley (2020) warns the first sign of trouble is your chicken may develop a "penguin stance." Your hens will lay fewer eggs and eventually stop laying eggs altogether.

Symptoms:
The hen lays a mass of rubbery solidified pus with a noticeable unpleasant smell.

Treatment:
If caught early, the condition can be treated with antibiotics.

SOFT EGGSHELLS

When the eggshell fails to be coated by calcium carbonate, the soft eggshell syndrome is the result. The most common cause of the condition is a lack of calcium in the chickens' diet.

Symptoms:
The egg is covered by a soft, malleable membrane only. The absence of shell is likely due to a dietary shortage.

Treatment:
You should add additional calcium, protein, and vitamins to your chickens' diet. Supplement your flock's feed with crushed oysters or eggshells by placing

these shells in a separate container for those hens who intuitively need it.

Check the feed you're using for your laying hens. It should be at least 16%-layer feed, and avoid giving these birds scraps while they're laying.

Bully stress may also cause soft shell syndrome. Remove the bully from the flock.

Young pullets sometimes lay soft-shelled eggs because their bodies have not yet reached the required level of maturity for the job. These birds will, in time, produce regular eggs.

EGG BINDING

When a hen can't lay the egg, her life becomes threatened, and immediate intervention is needed if the hens' life is saved.

The egg can become stuck between the cloaca (vent) and the uterus (shell gland) due to obesity, old age, or genetic dysfunction.

Symptoms:
Lesley (2020) warns the hen usually develops a penguin stance and pumps her tail to move the egg along.

Treatment
Where possible, seek veterinary advice.

Reasons:
− Lack of calcium in the diet
− Age
− Obesity
− Infection in the reproductive tract
− Stress
− Intestinal parasites
− Egg malformation
− Intentional retention of the egg may be due to no nesting box being available at the time of laying.

PROLAPSE

On rare occasions, hens may suffer a prolapse when the vent through which the egg was delivered does not retract into the body. This condition's telltale sign is a rather messy, wet bottom and a small piece of purple-colored flesh protruding from the vent. The other chickens may often peck at their sister's protruding flesh and cause her significant damage and pain.

Treatment
Treatment should begin as soon as you notice the problem. If you're able to manage the bird alone, hold your chicken firmly and clean away all the matted poop. You may need to cut away some feathers. Wash the area carefully with a mild disinfectant. Once the area around the vent has been cleaned, gently push the protruding flesh back into the internal canal, being very careful not to twist the oviduct tube as you work.

In most cases, you can safely push the tube back without any harm to the chicken. If, however, you feel unable to cope with the procedure, call your vet for assistance. Remove the affected chicken from the flock to avoid her being pecked.

Prognosis
Prolapses may happen in birds that started to lay at a young age, and the internal tissue has stretched and weakened as a result. If a hen strains to lay her eggs, a prolapse can result (Lesley, 2020b).

PASTY VENT

This health issue usually only affects young chicks but, if left unattended, can be life-threatening. Usually a stress-induced disorder, pasty vent effectively blocks feces' excretion, and the chicken can't pass droppings.

As soon as you notice your chicken has a crusted butt and appears lethargic and disinterested in food and water, act swiftly to treat the problem, or you'll lose your chicken! (Lesley, 2020b)

Treatment

Apply a warm, wet cloth to the chicken's messy area. Gently loosen the encrusted poop, and gradually the mess should start to soften and come away from the vent area. If the chick loses some feathers during the cleaning process, don't worry. Loss of a few feathers is better than the death of your bird. As soon as the vent is clean and clear of muck, pat the area dry, and your chick should be good to go (Lesley, 2020b).

EGG EATING

This strange behavior may be the result of insufficient calcium and protein in the chicken's diet.

Some chickens, when bored, will get into mischief and may eat eggs. On occasion, eggs are accidentally broken, and chickens find these delicious. Make sure to clean up any broken eggs as quickly as possible to avoid your chickens developing a taste for these tasty treats.

DISAPPEARING EGGS

You may notice that eggs suddenly disappear. The problem could be that the eggs are rolled away by rodents or swallowed by snakes. If opossums are the culprits, eggshells will be evident. Don't forget the human factor, too!

The best solution is to install a trail cam on the coop. However, snakes and rodents may bypass the device.

Rodent bait stations may work well as long as they're positioned out of other animals' reach.

Giant fishing nets may be effective in catching opossums.

As discussed previously, decoys or guard dogs can also work to offer protection.

BLOOD ON EGGS

Though eggs with blood smears may cause you alarm, there's often nothing much about which to worry.

A blood smear can be due to a small blood vessel rupture which generally heals quickly.

However, if you notice blood dripping from the chicken's vent area, remove her from the flock to avoid being pecked. Seek advice from your veterinarian if the bleeding doesn't stop.

STRANGE EGG SHELL COLORS

Eggshell color is a genetically controlled phenomenon that can also be affected by:

- Age
- Sunlight
- Stress
- Changes in temperature
- Molting
- If the egg spends too much time in the shell gland

ODD-SHAPED EGGS

Lesley (2020) reports that strangely shaped eggs are often due to a young hen's egg machinery not functioning fully.

Oddly shaped eggs may be classified as follows:

- Small eggs ("fart" eggs)
- Flat-sided eggs (slab eggs)
- Eggs with double yolks
- Eggs without the yolk

DISEASES

FOWL CHOLERA

Often more common in older cockerels than hens, Fowl Cholera affects the birds' joints, wattles, sinuses, and other body tissues. If left untreated, the disease will wipe out the oldest members of your flock in a matter of a week.

Symptoms (Beautyofbirds, 2020):

- Loss of appetite
- Greenish diarrhea
- Swollen, discolored wattles and comb
- Lameness due to swollen joints
- Nasal and oral discharge
- Gunky eyes

Treatment (Beautyofbirds, 2020):

Immediate antibiotic treatment is essential if you're to save your flock from death. Long-term treatment is advisable for chicken flocks that this disease has struck.

Improved sanitation and management of the cop, run, and feeding facilities are vital to avoid disease spread.

Intramuscular vaccinations with bacterins are also another form of treatment.

AVIAN INFLUENZA

Caused by a highly contagious, infectious, and deadly bird virus, avian influenza is usually spread to your flock by wild waterbirds. Infection is spread through saliva, feces, and mucus.

Symptoms (5M Editor, 2005):
- Diarrhea
- Wattle and comb edema and discoloration
- Nasal discharge
- Coughing and sneezing
- Ruffled feathers and shivering

Treatment (5M Editor, 2005):
Sadly, if your flock is infected with Avian Influenza, humane killing is often the best solution.

Due to the severity of this disease, all housing, equipment, and food will need to be destroyed as well.

To avoid such drastic measures, vaccination against AI is mandatory. Strict hygiene measures should be observed to prevent any diseases among your flock.

FOWL POX
This highly contagious viral avian pox comes in a wet and dry form.

Symptoms (Kathy, n.d.):
Distinctive wart-like growths on the wattles and comb

A significant decrease in egg production

Stunted growth in young birds

Treatment (Kathy, n.d.):
Remove the infected bird(s) from the flock and keep these in isolation in a special infirmary section.

Use antibiotics to treat any secondary infections.

Feed the affected birds with mashed eggs and a little chicken starter grower mash to avoid further discomfiture in the alimentary canal.

Supply plenty of clean, untreated water.

Treating the dry form of this disease with antibiotic cream can work wonders for alleviating the wart-like outbreaks.

Iodine dabbed onto infected areas can also help to sterilize the eye and mouth areas.

VetRx can be used to treat the wet form. This product will help soothe irritated airways.

Vaccination: Most day-old chicks from reputable suppliers have already been vaccinated.

COCCIDIOSIS
This highly infectious poultry disease is caused by **Coccidian protozoa** that live in the chicken's gut. The protozoa exit the stomach as sporocysts (egg-like structures) and infect the entire flock within a matter of a few hours.

Symptoms (Fox & Fox, 2018):
The sporocysts infect the chicken's gut lining damaging the gut walls and making these susceptible to infection.

- Loss of appetite
- Decreased growth rate
- Diarrhea
- The inability of nutrient absorption
- Significant weight loss
- Ruffled feathers
- Miserable-looking birds

Treatment (Fox & Fox, 2018):
Natural treatment remedies include garlic, neem, oregano, and green tea, to name a few.

Administer an anticoccidial drug.

Feed containing coccidiostat.

Ensure your chicken run has plenty of sunshine.

Dry out any damp areas as quickly as you can.

Remove damp bedding.

In high rainfall areas, lime the lawn regularly to limit the development of protozoans beneath the soil.

The chicken ingests protozoa-infested worms. Infection occurs immediately afterward. The challenge is to clean up all your chicken feces as quickly as possible to eradicate a further infestation.

Seek veterinary advice.

NEWCASTLE DISEASE

This rapidly spread disease can attack the respiratory, digestive, or nervous system causing untold damage and discomfiture to your chickens. Though the disease affects wild and domestic birds, it's particularly devastating to poultry.

Symptoms (Admin, 2019):
- Blood in the feces
- Diarrhea
- Lesions throughout the alimentary canal
- Hemorrhagic cloacitis (Bleeding from the cloaca)
- Loss of appetite
- Thick, blood mottled mucus around the beak or at the mouth corners
- Odd behavior
- Extreme contortion of the head and neck
- Leg paralysis

Treatment (Admin, 2019):

Commercial vaccines are available to treat Newcastle Disease, also known as Pneumoencephalitis.

The disease is spread via infected feces and contaminated saliva.

In addition to vaccinating, remove infected birds from the flock and isolate them until they're fully recovered.

Thoroughly clean the run and coop. Ensure all feed and water containers are washed in hot water with white vinegar that acts as a mild, nontoxic disinfectant.

Substitute all bedding with fresh dry straw or pine needles.

Ensure your chickens have minimum contact with wild birds.

Manage feeding and water stations with extreme diligence.

SALMONELLOSIS

Salmonellosis, caused by bacterial disease carried by rodents, can result in enteritis and septicemia.

Symptoms (LLC, 2021):
- Chalky diarrhea
- Pasty vent
- Loss of appetite
- Closed eyes
- Significant weight loss
- Intense thirst
- Ruffled feathers
- Dejection

Treatment (LLC, 2021):

Salmonellosis can be transmitted from hen to chick or via soil, bedding water, or feeder contamination.

Supportive care: Remove the infected bird from the flock. Place it in a warm, safe location with food and water. Call your vet.

Antibiotics are the usual course of treatment.

Adding prebiotics and probiotics, thyme, turmeric, and ashwagandha to feed can offer support against salmonellosis. Extreme hygiene in the run and coop is essential.

MEDICATED FEEDS

Just as you need medication from time to time when you're ill, your chickens will benefit from more than healthy, clean living conditions when they fall prey to disease. As an excellent preventative measure against certain diseases, many good brands of poultry feed have medicinal additives.

The two most common medications added to poultry feed include coccidiostats and antibiotics, which reputable feed manufacturers usually supply. Some examples of coccidiostats added to poultry rations include amprolium, monensin sodium, salinomycin, and lasalocid (Agriculture.com Staff, 2018).

Because preventing coccidiosis by improving sanitation alone can be challenging, constant low coccidiostats doses will help maintain a healthy flock free of this unpleasant disease. Mature chickens usually develop an immunity to the disease if they're fed a mild amount of coccidiostats until they're 16 weeks old.

Antibiotics added in prophylactic levels to poultry feeds help maintain the flock's good health by preventing several minor diseases that can lower egg-laying production and, if left untreated, decimate your entire chicken flock (Agriculture.com Staff, 2018).

INJURIES

Whether you like it or not, injuries among your chickens are a given. These wounds may be due to bullying, pecking, a dog attack, or parasites. The challenge you face is to check the bird's entire body beneath the feathers for any lesions, wounds, and bleeding.

Once you've located the wounds, cut away feathers in the region to allow better access to the injury site. Cleanse the area well with a weak solution of hydrogen peroxide. You may want to use Blu-Kote that helps seal the wound. Raw honey also works well as a wound-healing agent.

Depending on the severity of the wound, treatment twice a day has the best results.

Bandaging wounds isn't advisable, as the chickens simply scratch off the covering and may further injure themselves.

If in doubt, contact your veterinarian for further advice and support.

Isolation Pen

Remove the injured bird from the flock as soon as you notice there's a problem. You may not know what's ailing your chicken, so it's best to err on the side of caution by placing the sick or injured bird into a smaller pen for observation and treatment. Isolation will help protect the chicken from pecking and bullying by the other chickens.

Ensure the isolation area is warm, dry, and has adequate cover protection from flies. Flies are notoriously attracted to blood and ailing chickens (CuzChickens, 2016).

Feeding Sickly or Injured Chickens

Regular feeding is advisable. However, if your bird has lost a lot of blood, add electrolytes and vitamins to the clean water. Sav-A-Chick and Nutri-Drench work particularly well for injured chickens (CuzChickens, 2016).

If you can't get to the store for supplies, CuzChickens (2016) recommends a mixture of cup sugar and one tablespoon baking soda added to a gallon of boiled water. Allow the mixture to cool and give it to your injured chicken; they should perk up quickly after that.

Reintroduction to the Flock
Once the wound has completely covered and your chicken is perky and eating well, put it back with the flock. Keep a watchful eye on how the chicken settles in. There will be some argumentative behavior, as the pecking order may need to be reconfirmed.

CHICKEN FIRST AID KIT

As with your family and other pets, illness, injuries, and allergy issues arise from time to time. Best be prepared for similar incidents among your chickens and have a chicken first aid kit on hand to deal with these emergencies.

Prepare a particular sick bay area that can double as a maternity ward or isolation space for aggressive flock members.

First Aid Essentials
These will include a wound cleaner, disposable gloves, nonstick gauze, scissors, tweezers, dog nail clippers for beak trimming, superglue gel for beak repairs, and an LED headlamp. Epsom salts and a small tub (suitable for soaking chickens' feet) are also helpful.

Added to the above items, ensure your first aid kit has the following:

- Aspirin
- Neosporin ointment
- Styptic powder for bleeding beaks and claws
- Popsicle stick for splints
- Liquid calcium
- Tea bags for beak repair
- Old towels for wrapping sickly chickens
- Dog training floor pads for padding for sick birds
- Porzyme for nutritional and digestive support
- A chicken saddle for over-mating feather loss
- Lafeber's Nutri-Start Hand Feeding Formula for chickens that are too ill to eat on their own
- Electrolyte solution
- Chlorhexidine 2% antibacterial solution for cleaning and disinfecting wounds
- Make sure you have the contact details for the closest avian veterinarian in your area.

Homemade Electrolyte Solution
Mormino (2012) suggests you always keep this solution on hand in case of emergencies.

Ingredients:
- 1 teaspoon potassium chloride (if you don't have this product, omit it from the recipe)
- 1 teaspoon sodium bicarbonate (baking soda)
- 1 teaspoon sodium chloride (table salt)
- 1 tablespoon sucrose (sugar)
- 1 gallon of boiled water

Method
- Boil the water
- Stir in all the ingredients
- Allow cooling
- Administer to dehydrated chickens in place of drinking water for four to six hours, then provide normal water for the bird's needs.

Overheating
When your chickens become overheated due to hot weather or poor ventilation in the coop, this electrolytic solution works well to restore the birds' mineral balance.

Provide garden sprinklers for your chickens to help reduce the effects of heat stress. You'll enjoy watching their antics as they run through the spraying water as happy kids (Mormino, 2012).

THE IMPORTANCE OF LIGHTING IN THE COOP

Lighting for your backyard chicken flock is more critical than you may imagine. Chickens absorb light through the top of their skull as well as their eyes. Chickens have four cone color receptors, which see red, blue, green, and ultraviolet light. Humans only have the first three types of cones in the retinas of their eyes. According to Johnson (2018), chickens respond well to a programmed day-night cycle that positively affects their growth development, natural immunity, general health, and reproductive cycle.

Using LED lights on a timer in your chicken coop will effectively raise egg production. Bear in mind that, like you, your chickens need time to sleep, so lights will turn off at a prescheduled time to allow the birds to catch some much-needed shut-eye.

Depending on the scale of your flock and your intentions about a commercially viable enterprise, it will directly influence your need to install lighting in your chicken coop. For most beginner backyard chicken keepers, leaving your flock just as it is might be perfectly sufficient for their needs and yours (Johnson, 2018).

THE NEXT STEP

Paying close attention to your chickens and studying their behaviors will quickly give you a warning if one of them isn't feeling well, and you can respond accordingly (Lesley, 2020).

Now, let's take a look at the importance of using the correct litter and managing your coop's hygiene to ensure the best possible results for a healthy, productive flock.

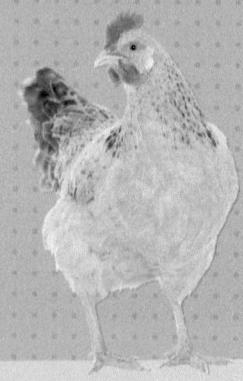

5 UNDERSTANDING THE IMPORTANCE OF CHICKEN LITTER MANAGEMENT

You might never have considered the importance of managing your chickens' litter. After all, wastage is unpleasant and should be disposed of as quickly as possible. Although this is true, successful management of your flock's litter can be the difference between life and death.

Strange though it may sound, composting litter correctly will ensure a healthier flock as well as a more hygienic coop.

Litter represents your chickens' "calling card." When you learn to identify what regular litter looks like, you'll be quick to notice any changes that possibly indicate a sickly flock member.

THE SCOOP ON POOP MANAGEMENT

For optimum success with litter management, the litter should be dry (Banrie, 2012). Litter conditions directly impact your chickens' performance which, in turn, will affect production and profits.

When conditions in the coop become damp and the ventilation is poor, poop becomes wet and begins to cake onto your chickens' feet and various other places in the enclosure. You may notice the caked poop around the water dispensers, feeders, nesting boxes, and roosting perches. If this is the case, the coop needs an urgent cleaning. The increase in ammonia levels due to wet litter can have a profoundly negative health effect on both your flock and you. High levels of ammonia are believed to affect egg-laying performance and adversely impact your broilers' growth and development.

Adequate ventilation is essential for drying out the litter. However, excessive ventilation may cause draughts, which will chill your chicks, resulting in other health complications. There's a fine line between maintaining good airflow without stressing the flock.

Normal Dry Litter

Partially dry and ranging through a series of shades from brown to gray, regular poultry litter usually crumbles easily and is almost entirely ammonia-free.

Maintaining dry manure, which consists of bedding material, loose feathers, and poop, is essential for controlling ammonia levels and ensuring your flock's health is not negatively impacted by the excessive gas release.

Litter buildup may go unnoticed to the beginner chicken keeper, so be warned at the outset of your venture to remove litter buildup before the problem escalates. During the hot weather, your chickens will potentially consume several gallons of water per day.

A percentage of the water is passed through the body, which may cause the litter to cake. Inadequate ventilation in the coop can exacerbate the problem. Damp, caked litter is the springboard for the buildup of toxic ammonia gas.

Abnormal Litter

Abnormal litter can range through white, yellow, orange, green, and in severe cases, it may be bloody, watery, or sticky. Sickly poultry can usually be identified by the color and consistency of their litter.

However, abnormal manure is not only a sign of diseased birds. It also increases the potential for the spread of disease and the buildup of ammonia, both of which are harmful to your flock.

Added to this fact, wet litter begins to clump and adheres to surfaces in the coop, the chicken run, and your chickens' feet. If not speedily managed, the entire area will soon become encrusted with foul-smelling chicken feces.

An increase in the ammonia levels in your chicken coop is often easy to detect, as the smell alone is likely to make you gasp for breath. If your coop poop levels have reached this point, you can only imagine how uncomfortable your chickens feel.

However, relying on your sense of smell alone is no guarantee for ammonia detection. Should you become desensitized to the smell, you're unlikely to notice an increase in ammonia levels. For this reason, adequate ventilation of the coop and amendments to litter control are two vital practices to keep in mind.

Though costly, investing in ammonia sensors may help to alert you when these levels rise, thus giving you time to eradicate the problem before your chickens suffer the consequences of the elevated ammonia levels (Banrie, 2012). For beginner chicken keepers with smaller flocks, simple house cleaning should suffice.

Litter pH affects ammonia levels. Some chicken keepers treat their flock's litter with acidifying agents to lower the pH to below seven before introducing a new flock of chickens. However, maintaining the ideal pH level is challenging because the treatment only lasts 10–14 days. To be effective, the procedure should be regularly repeated, which becomes impractical when the flock is in the coop (Banrie, 2012).

Maintaining reasonable control over your chickens' manure provides a healthier environment in which your chickens are less likely to succumb to acid burns on their hocks and footpads. Breast blistering will also be significantly reduced when litter is managed correctly. Thus, good litter management is beneficial not only to your flock but to everyone who works with your birds (Banrie, 2012).

Fan installation can be a lucrative, though costly, management tool. However, with rising fuel costs, this is unlikely to be a sensible option for the beginner backyard chicken keeper. Thus, your best choice is to ensure you keep your coop clean and well-ventilated. Remain alert to changes in your feathered friends' poop and respond immediately.

The trick, says Banrie (2012), is to stay ahead of the problem by maintaining the best routine practices possible to ensure your flock's optimum health and well-being.

IN-HOUSE WINDROWING

If you've invested in a larger flock, this type of litter management between rows in broiler houses is essential for the optimum healthy environment of your chickens.

The rows of litter between flocks are mechanically shoveled, plowed, and piled in rows down the center of the henhouse. As the bacteria's natural metabolism begins, heat is generated in the rows of litter. Gradually the heat increases to between 140 and 160 °F, and it effectively destroys harmful microorganisms and pathogens such as *Salmonella* and E. Coli that are usually found in chicken poop.

Some chicken keepers believe it best to remove the caked litter before windrowing. However, not only is this a time-consuming and potentially costly exercise, the caked litter that is mixed into the litter pile will help generate sufficient heat for the success of the entire process (5M Editor, 2009).

Regularly turning the manure stacks helps ensure good air circulation through the composting material and allows for the even distribution of heat throughout the entire pile.

Depending on the area to be windrowed and the stack size, the process can take up to seven days from start to finish. Well-conditioned windrowed litter should then be flattened and spread out to allow any remaining ammonia to be expelled in preparation for the arrival of the next batch of new chicks.

PARTIAL HOUSE CLEANING

Banrie (2012) warns keeping litter dry is your primary concern. Reusing or reprocessing used waste is quite another story.

The partial house cleaning waste management method involves removing a large amount of waste from the center of the coop and redistributing the remaining waste throughout the enclosure. In some instances, and depending on the size of your coop and flock, a partial cleaning might be more cost-effective than you imagined.

However, as the cost of bedding and litter material escalates, so does the environmental concern for dumping litter. There are often strict bylaws governing waste dumping. These rules may have a negative backlash for you and your backyard flock.

Ensure you understand the laws in your state or urban zone about waste management to avoid falling foul of the law.

Often, the best solution is to till as much of the composted litter into your garden, where it'll help to produce succulent fruits and vegetables. That way, your backyard chicken enterprise has a positive and sustainable knock-on environmental effect.

DROPPING BOARDS

Managing your flock's waste depends on which method works best for you. Mormino (2013b) suggests some chicken keepers prefer to have a minimum buildup of litter waste in the coop as possible. They like to regularly clean out their coop, thus ensuring a minimum of waste buildup and their flock's maximum health. For some of these keepers, dropping boards have proved a valuable and reliable method of managing waste.

Dropping boards are shelf-like structures laid below the roost and are designed to your chickens' dripping vent while they're asleep. The boards are easy to slide out, clean off, and replace, thus saving you time and keeping the bedding area a lot cleaner.

This waste management method is both cost-effective and easy to implement and may, therefore, suit beginner chicken keepers quite well.

The Benefits of Dropping Boards Include (Mormino, 2012a):

1. Keeping the nighttime buildup of poop more manageable to clean.
2. Less frequent litter change is necessary.
3. The boards save time and therefore money.
4. They reduce flies.
5. The dropping boards help to reduce ammonia buildup.
6. You should never compromise your chickens' health.
7. The boards can reduce the risk of frostbite during the winter months.

DEEP LITTER METHOD

The deep litter method of waste management may seem to go against what was previously discussed above about keeping your henhouse clean. However, this system works well when chicken waste is allowed to pile up inside the coop. You might think this sounds awful, right?

The method works as a deep mulch system in which layer upon layer of litter waste is laid on each other to create a fully functional composting heap inside the coop. At the bottom of the pile, the oldest bedding begins to disintegrate and turn into beneficial compost.

Much like your garden compost system, the deep litter method adds layers of waste, which your chickens then manage by scratching, pecking, and picking at the bedding, thus turning the material throughout the day. In the process, the waste is aerated and dries out. The process encourages healthy, harmless parasites that feed on the chicken waste causing it to break down into useful compost. The deep litter method alleviates the costly problem of cleaning the coop every week and substituting expensive bedding. In effect, the process saves you time and money.

The chicken poop is rich in nitrogen, so you need to layer carbonaceous material to balance composting's chemical process. Chelsea Green Publishing (2020) recommends the higher the carbon component of the deep litter method, the better.

The secret of this clever way to manage your chickens' waste is to start with a good layer of pine shavings, which effectively absorb nitrogen from the poop, reduce the smell, and create valuable humus, or the dark and spongy substance in soil, for use in your veggie patch and garden.

SIGNS THAT THE DEEP LITTER METHOD IS WORKING

Though the process may sound unpleasant and off-putting, the deep litter method has many positive attributes. Among these are the following.

Neutral Odor

If your deep litter method is functioning correctly, there shouldn't be any noticeable or nasty smell in the coop. The aeration process ensures gasses are released, and the valuable parasites are doing their job in munching through the decaying matter.

Cuts Down the Pest Population

A well-managed deep litter system ensures fly and mosquito numbers inside the coop drop significantly by becoming prey for the good parasites in the compost.

Calm, Happy Chickens

Busy chickens are happy chickens, and keeping your flock comfortable means they'll suffer less stress. Chickens love to be kept busy scratching, pecking, and picking. A deep litter compost system will keep your birds entertained as they poke around for tasty critters hiding in the composting material. Thus, feather pulling, bullying, and social disputes should begin to drop off.

Smith (2020) reckons the deep litter method is one of the most straightforward, reliable, and suitable litter management systems you can use. Though your busy, attentive flock members will do most of the work in regularly turning the litter over, all you need do is keep a watchful eye out for areas the birds may have missed. Not too difficult! What do you say?

Fantastic Compost at Your Fingertips

The fantastic thing about the deep litter method is that you'll have the richest, most nutritious compost for your vegetable garden after a time, and you didn't have to dig and till that much.

Saves Time and Money

You're sure to agree there's merit in the deep litter method. With costs soaring and time becoming an expensive commodity, your thrifty, sweet chickens are going to save you time and money while providing your food needs and great compost for your garden.

WHERE TO BEGIN

When you prepare for your new chickens, generously spread the clean floor with suitable pine shavings or hemp bedding. Then, introduce your beloved chickens to their new coop. The best time to do this is when the weather warms up. If you're living in a four-season region, this can correspond to spring.

There are several other types of litter that work well in the deep litter method. These include peanut shells, crushed corn cobs, hay, pine or hardwood chips, rice hulls, and nontoxic processed shredded paper. Once you have the litter prepared, you can introduce your beloved chickens to their new coop.

As time passes, the chickens will scratch their droppings and other waste material into the shavings to create a well-turned composting layer. The warmth from the natural chemical composting process will ensure your flock is snug throughout the colder months.

Stir the bedding regularly to break down any clumps of manure and ensure all the particles are well-mixed. Add more bedding, grass clippings, and pine shavings as the layers are compacted.

You may want to try scattering some corn treats onto the bedding to further encourage your birds to scratch and turn the waste material.

Smith (2020) recommends cleaning out the coop every six months. Leave a small, thin layer of the old material behind to start the composting process again. This starting layer is sometimes called the "mother layer" (Smith, 2020).

REQUIREMENTS FOR THE DEEP LITTER METHOD

When implementing the deep litter method, remember these tips for success (Mormino, 2013b):

1. Use a carbon-based litter material such as pine shavings, pine needles, leaves, and grass clippings.
2. Nitrogen-rich chicken droppings: Chicken manure is rich in nitrogen, phosphorus, and potassium. For this reason, manure makes the best compost.
3. Oxygen: Good aeration of the litter pile is essential for the composting process to work. Make sure to manually turn any caked areas, especially those near the water and feed containers.
4. Maintaining a viable moisture balance for successful composting without the waste material molding and rotting is essential.
5. Good ventilation is essential for removing ammonia gases and excessive moisture.

VALUABLE TIPS TO KEEP IN MIND FOR THE DEEP LITTER METHOD

1. Start the litter building process when the weather begins to warm so that the litter pile will generate adequate heat through the colder months of the year.
2. Start by laying four to six inches of pine shavings.
3. Maintain a litter depth of at least six inches. Add more litter as the pile dwindles.

4. Aerate the litter regularly. Though the chickens will do a great job, pay attention to those areas they'll have missed.
5. Break up caked areas.
6. Mix the litter well into the bedding to avoid clumping.
7. From time to time, squeeze a handful of litter. If it clumps and balls, add more shavings to soak up the extra moisture. If the chicken litter crumbles quickly, it's too dry and will need a little water stirred in.
8. Remove some litter periodically to maintain the six-inch level.
9. Keep the waterers outside the coop.
10. Coops with concrete floors are easier to clean and disinfect but are colder during winter. Earth floors are challenging to clean, sometimes clumping when wet and difficult to disinfect.
11. Esmail (2011) suggests the challenge with keeping your coop clean and functionally will always be the complete removal of infectious and germ-filled wet litter and debris. The ongoing problems caused by poorly constructed cages that leak condensation onto the litter are an essential aspect to bear in mind when building your coop and run.
12. The timely replacement of equipment is essential for the overall success of your backyard venture. Mending water leaks and replacing ineffective nipples on the waterers will help avoid the buildup of caking, which will eventually ruin the deep litter method.
13. Adequate ventilation is essential for the deep litter method to be a successful enterprise.
14. To kick-start the following year's composting process, leave a little of the old litter when you clear out the coop each spring.

ADVANTAGES AND DISADVANTAGES OF LITTER MATERIALS

According to Esmail (2011), it's essential to be aware of the types of litter you use in the deep litter method, as some of these are more beneficial than others.

Here is a list of the pros and cons of various litter materials:

Advantages and Disadvantages of Litter Materials

Material	Advantages	Disadvantages
Peanut hulls	Inexpensive and easy to obtain	Molds easily and may have pesticide residues
Pine and hardwood chips	Successful when dry	May cause breast blistering when wet
Rice hulls	Successful when available at a reasonable price	Chicks may eat the hulls
Nontoxic Processed paper	Excellent litter material	It can cause caking and requires close management
Crushed corn cobs	Successful when dry	Can cause breast blistering when wet
Sand	Readily available, inexpensive, and easy to clean	Difficult to maintain sustainable temperatures during winter months and requires excellent ventilation to maintain dryness.
Cropped straw or hay	Readily available, affordable, and warm when dry	It tends to mold when wet, which creates unhealthy respiratory conditions for the flock.

WARNING

Remove all the litter if your flock suffers from any disease. Hose the coop down and thoroughly disinfect the entire area and everything inside the enclosure before reintroducing a new litter layer and your brood of chickens once the health issue has been solved.

THE POTENTIAL DANGERS OF THE DEEP LITTER METHOD

There are numerous dangers to keep in mind when beginning the deep litter method (Esmail, 2011):

1. Don't use chemicals or diatomaceous earth as a starter, as this will kill off all the good bacteria needed for successful composting.
2. Avoid using hay or straw for the starter layer, as these natural media mold quickly and cause respiratory problems for your flock. This result is perhaps the most severe drawback of the deep litter method when it's poorly managed.
3. Don't allow the ammonia odor to build up, as it causes respiratory and eye irritations in your chickens.
4. Remove all wet bedding, as this promotes the growth of mold, harmful bacteria, and coccidiosis. Chickens can suffer from bumblefoot from damp litter.
5. Don't overcrowd the coop.
6. Avoid the coop's regular cleaning, as this action defeats the whole composting process of the deep litter method.
7. Chickens kept on the floor come into direct and constant contact with their feces which can cause a number of health issues for your flock if not adequately managed.

Mormino (2013b) warns that the deep litter method can become a nightmare when unsuccessfully managed. Toxic ammonia gases are produced. Harmful bacteria and *Capillaria* worms can become a problem.

Deep litter that's too dry will cause noxious dust filled with harmful airborne spores that will adversely affect your flock's respiratory health.

If in doubt about using the deep litter method, rather be safe than sorry. Choose a litter system you'll find manageable and do the composting outside the coop (Smith, 2020).

THE NEXT STEP

As a chicken keeper, you'll want to ensure you offer your feathered family the best care. Apart from giving them healthy feed, a warm and safe place to live and sleep, as well as adequate space to lay their tasty eggs, you need to have a good routine in place.

Like many other domestic animals, chickens are routine driven. They wake at dawn and prepare to roost at sunset. In between times, they eat, drink, scratch, forage, play, lay eggs, and do all their other daily chicken chores.

With that in mind, let's now take a look at just how important routine is for your beloved chooks.

6. ROUTINE IS KEY TO YOUR SUCCESS

Now that you understand the importance of chicken health, safety, and nutrition, you need to set up a good routine. Your daily, weekly, and monthly activities should ensure that your precious backyard flock is kept healthy, safe, and well-nourished.

Much like looking after your home and family, your chickens need regular tending to keep them happy, healthy, and productive.

In all aspects of your backyard chicken-keeping venture, keep things simple. The less complicated your plans, the easier these will be to implement with tremendous success.

Some first-time chicken keepers are easily overwhelmed by the excitement of bringing home their delightful, tiny, heart-melting chicks. All is good and well for the first few days, and things can sometimes go somewhat cockeyed. It's at times such as these that routines, dreaded by some and adored by others, should be instituted.

For ease of management, essential and suggested routine tasks have been listed below. Let's take a look at these vital functions and discuss each of them in more detail.

DAILY ACTIVITIES

Specific daily tasks are an absolute, vital necessity if your chicken flock is to remain healthy and happy, and you're to stay calm and stress-free!

WATER CHECK

Besides air, clean water is an essential life-giving element for all living creatures. As has already been mentioned, chickens are thirsty animals that drink a lot more water than you might imagine. The birds will quickly dehydrate if they don't have enough clean water. Like you, your chickens won't drink dirty or contaminated water. Hence, your first responsibility each morning will be to ensure your flock has plenty of fresh, clean water.

Water can quickly become contaminated by droppings, bedding, shavings, and other bits of debris that the chickens inadvertently scratch and kick around. Depending on your flock's size, you may need to refresh the water containers more than once during the day.

Ensure the water containers are well-cleaned to remove any slime or algae residue that may have formed along the inner edges. Use your usual dish detergent and plenty of hot water for the task. If you use oxygenated or chlorine bleach to sanitize your flock's water containers, make sure to rinse these containers well before refilling these with fresh, clean water.

In an attempt to keep water containers as clean as possible, consider raising these off the ground by about four to six inches. The raised container simply allows your hens a little more scratching space with less debris flung into the water. Keeping the water containers outside the coop may also help to reduce water contamination.

You may want to consider installing an automated drinking system as a potential solution. Although these items are costly, there's sure to be a model best suited to your needs. Most automated and computerized systems protect the water from contamination by allowing the chickens to drink from nipples instead of from an open watering container.

However, beginner chicken keepers usually farm with smaller flocks that may require less sophisticated equipment. Plastic containers suspended above floor level, within easy reach for chickens to drink from, often work quite satisfactorily.

That said, the availability of clean, fresh water is paramount to your flock's health. No matter your watering system's choice, the equipment's optimum cleanliness is essential (Williams, 2020).

FEEDING

Feeding your precious backyard flock runs a close second to catering for their hydration needs. Get the feeding program right, and you'll have happy, healthy, productive chickens that welcome you with cheerful clucks each time you bring tasty snacks and delicious scraps. There's little to beat the sound of a contented chicken welcome!

Finding the best supplies for your hungry brood can be somewhat of a challenge. Do these birds eat the same food you do? Can they be given fruits and veggies? What about bread and baked goods?

For starters, though your feathered girls have the capacity to eat like gannets, careful consideration must be given to their diet. What you really need is a healthy flock of productive egg layers or chubby broilers instead of sickly, overweight birds that have lost interest in life.

Here's some excellent advice for the most nutritious diet that can help you get the feeding program just right for your backyard flock.

WHAT TO FEED YOUR CHICKENS

Claire (2015) recommends a core diet of high-quality, organic chicken feed with a good balance of protein and vitamins. You can add maize, oats, sunflower seeds, and wheat for variety, which is sure to keep your feathered family happy.

Table and kitchen scraps often go down a treat with your flock. Just remember not to include fatty or salty foods among the tidbits. Chickens generally love vegetables and fruit, especially apple cores, grated carrots, carrot leaves, and spinach. Your girls are likely to love you dearly if you treat them to bananas or melons. Some chickens will also gobble pizza, porridge, and pasta scrap, says Claire (2015).

TREATS

As previously mentioned in chapter three, special treats and snacks should be healthy choices for special occasions. Remember, treats don't take the place of regular meals. Dried mealworms are usually an absolute triumph! Your flock will love these high-protein treats. Other healthy treats include pumpkin, apples, porridge (in winter), and broccoli (Claire, 2015).

FOODS TO AVOID

As previously mentioned, Claire (2015) also warns that you should avoid feeding your precious chickens raw green peels, especially those from green potatoes. Potatoes are part of the nightshade family of plants, and as such, their green peels contain a highly toxic steroidal alkaloid called solanine. Harmful to both humans and animals, green potato skins and potato "eyes" should be avoided as they cause severe gastrointestinal and neurological disorders.

Although not toxic to chickens, citrus fruits have a high acidic content unsuitable for your flock when eaten in large quantities.

All processed foods, which usually have a high sodium content, shouldn't be included in your chickens' diet.

HOW TO FEED YOUR FLOCK

Your backyard chickens are likely kept in a hen run, coop, or pen. If this is the case, avoid contaminating the food by throwing it onto the ground among the bird's droppings.

The decision to use a hanging feeder, a closed container treadle feeder, or an open container will depend on the size of your flock.

Once again, open feeding systems are more easily contaminated by your busy, overzealous birds scratching and pecking at the food. By introducing a closed feeding system, you cut down wastage as well as feed contamination.

Each day, check on the quantity of feed in the containers you've chosen to use. Make sure the chickens' feed is well-preserved, with no mold or dampness. Ensure the feeding slots are clean and free of clumped wet food.

Because chickens thrive on variety and simple challenges, having a hanging feeder in one area and a treadle feeder in another is sure to encourage your busy, intelligent flock members to figure out ways to use both methods successfully.

WHEN TO FEED YOUR FLOCK

Feeding should be done during the day only. Avoid nighttime feeding as this tends to attract rodents. The more you interact with your flock, the better you'll know how much to feed these busy, chatty family members.

To avoid attracting flies, make sure that you clean up well after the girls once they have enjoyed eating scraps. In their excitement, your birds will have kicked and scratched up quite a storm, leaving remnants that will mold, rot, and become delicious snacks for unpleasant, disease-carrying pests.

You may want to have food available throughout the day, or perhaps you prefer to feed your chickens only twice a day. Whichever method you decide to use, make sure the feed is fresh and edible.

If you're working away from home, feeding morning and evening will probably work best for you. However, if you're at home with your flock, you'll enjoy feeding a little food three to five times a day.

Ensure the food is shared and that the dominant birds don't gobble everything. If this event becomes a challenge, feed the weaker birds separately to ensure they get their fill.

WARNING

It's illegal to feed your chickens on chicken carcasses because this action may increase the risk of contamination of your flock with chicken diseases. Though no one is likely to know if you choose to feed your birds the odd bit of leftover chicken from the table, for health reasons, no animal should be fed meat from an animal of the same species (Claire, 2015).

In the case of dead chickens, burying carcasses isn't always the best solution, as these can be dug up by hungry predators, thus spreading potential disease among their own kind. Dispose of dead flock members by incinerating the carcasses, thus ensuring no other animals are contaminated by potentially diseased food.

EGG COLLECTING

Whether you're a small-time backyard chicken farmer who wants to sell eggs to the local market or simply providing good wholesome food for your own family, fresh, clean eggs are a must.

Gathering the eggs early in the morning is the best practice. This way, the eggs are less likely to have been pooped on and require no added cleaning.

Collecting eggs daily ensures optimal freshness and less chance of shells being cracked or damaged. Eggs left in the nesting boxes become soiled and difficult to clean (Arcuri, 2020a).

CHICKEN WATCH

Most pets like attention, and so do your chickens. Spending time with these productive girls will keep you in the loop of their behavior patterns. You'll quickly notice if one chicken appears out of sorts or if there's any bullying on the go. It's also easier to find health problems by understanding chickens based on their unique personalities. Happy, busy, and bright-eyed birds are those that are in peak health.

Watch out for any signs of frustration, isolation, or injury among the members of your flock. Also, monitor each bird's eating and drinking habits. As mentioned above, remove the bully birds if they're stopping the rest of the pullets from eating, drinking, and going about their regular daily chicken business.

All in all, like any good chicken keeper, you need to know as much as possible about your flock to maintain their good health and productivity. In return, your chickens will enjoy your company and run over to give you a heartwarming welcome each time you visit. Added to this welcome, you'll be rewarded with fresh eggs daily!

WEEKLY ACTIVITIES

COOP CLEANING AND MAINTENANCE
The dreaded housework never ends! You've no doubt heard this sort of comment often enough, and your chicken coop is no exception.

Keeping the coop clean and free from rotting food, clumps of wet feces, and in good general repair will ensure your flock's health and safety. In the long run, your attention to small details will potentially save you time and money.

Your flock will likely enjoy the attention to their living quarters, as not only do they get to spend time with you, they'll scratch alongside you, offering their support and help with the task of cleaning up.

MONTHLY ACTIVITIES

BEDDING MANAGEMENT
Depending on your location, the size of your flock, and the type of bedding you've laid down for your chickens, changing the bedding will need to be done at different times during the year.

The deep litter method may need to be changed once or twice a year.

Check your flock's bedding and remove any rotting molding materials as soon as you notice these. Add new layers of shaving, grass cuttings, and other suitable bedding material when necessary.

NESTING BOX CLEANUP
Keep the nesting boxes clear of broken shells, poop, and wet decaying matter. Though you'll remove noticeable items daily when you collect eggs, a good sprucing up of your chickens' nesting boxes will make your girls feel much more comfortable.

WATERER SANITIZATION
As previously mentioned, one of the most critical health hazards for your chickens is dirty, blocked, or contaminated waterers. Make it your monthly priority to clean and disinfect these waterers, especially the nozzles if you use these. Scrub down the units with a weak bleach solution and plenty of hot water. Rinse the unit well before refilling it (Walker, 2017).

PREPARATION FOR WEATHER CHANGES
Walker (2017) suggests your chickens will need a little extra warmth and care as the colder months approach. Plan well ahead to ensure their coop is dry and snug. Weatherproof the roof against snow and rain. Extra padding in the nesting boxes and snug roosting space should also be provided.

Added lighting will encourage your girls to continue laying during the dark, cold months.

If you live in a country where the winter months are particularly challenging, stock up the supplies you'll need to see your flock safely through this period. By being well-prepared, you'll be confident that your chickens will have everything they need to keep them happy. Just as small children get frustrated when they believe there's nothing much to occupy them, your chickens may become exasperated during the winter. Don't forget the little extra tidbits to alleviate the boredom during the weeks when your birds are stuck in the coop due to bad weather.

Make sure you have the extra feed, crushed oyster shells, grit, and bales of fresh pine shavings ready for the flock. Watch out for product specials and interesting new supplies that may benefit your chickens.

SANITIZE THE COOP
Sanitizing the coop is clearly one of the most challenging tasks you will face. Not only will your flock need to be moved into their run, which they may not enjoy, but you should also tackle this job on a warm day when the girls will enjoy the sunshine and the chance to stretch their little legs.

As previously mentioned, sanitizing the entire coop, run, and all the chicken furniture and equipment is a huge task. You may want to enlist the family's help and enjoy picnicking in the chicken run with your greedy brood wanting to share every morsel with you! It could turn out to be a fun day!

Remember to clean out all the corners where muck may have accumulated and use a safe sanitizer (diluted bleach solution) for the job. Though not every chicken keeper prefers it, diatomaceous earth can be sprinkled over the floor area to kill off mites and other unpleasant critters. Pine shavings and needles can be used instead.

OTHER IMPORTANT RECURRING TASKS

Though it's an enjoyable and thoroughly rewarding job, keeping your backyard flock in good health takes time and effort, which you'll discover is all worthwhile in the end.

Keep a detailed roster of all the chores you need to accomplish during the days, weeks, and months ahead. Maintaining a good routine year-round will ensure your flock stays happy, healthy, and productive while you feel confident about taking good care of their needs.

Keep the chicken first aid kit well-stocked. Replenish and replace medications that have expired (Melissa, 2012).

TIPS FOR FULL-TIME CHICKEN KEEPERS

You may be wondering if you'll cope raising backyard chickens while having to work all day. The answer is a resounding YES!

Setting up and getting your flock settled and acclimatized is your greatest challenge. You could perhaps tackle this task when you're on leave or over a weekend.

All you need is a small flock of about five or six chickens and adequate space to keep the birds safe, warm, and dry. An enclosed, predator-proof pen with a sheltered area is ideal (Steele, 2017).

Allow your flock out of the coop early each morning before you leave for work. If you leave home before the sun comes up, you may want to install an automated door that will spring open at sunrise. The door can work in reverse at the end of the day if you're not home to shut the brood in for the night.

Make sure the birds have food and fresh water. During hotter months, ensure there's plenty of water, as chickens will drink more than they eat during summer. The last thing you need is dehydrated hens, so copious amounts of fresh water are an absolute must.

Egg collection will probably have to be done at night if your day starts earlier than sunrise.

Make your weekends your priority time in caring for the chickens with the whole family. Not only will you find this rewarding and therapeutic, but the chickens will love the company, too (Steele, 2017).

THE NEXT STEP

Now that you have a good idea of the routines required for backyard chicken keeping, it's time to prepare for weather and temperature changes. As previously mentioned, keeping your flock well-hydrated and fed are only two essential aspects of chicken keeping. Warmth and ventilation play a vital role in the overall well-being and productivity of your chickens.

7. THE IMPACT OF WEATHER AND TEMPERATURE ON YOUR FLOCK

As a beginner chicken keeper, you'll possibly be wondering how to help your small flock survive extreme weather changes. You may, in fact, feel quite unsettled about how best to protect your precious chickens in the event of a flood, hurricane, or tornado.

This chapter deals with inclement weather conditions and will give you tips on how you can best safeguard your flock during these sometimes unexpected but certainly traumatic and often life-threatening events.

Climate change plays a vital role in animal and food production. The increased heat is one of the single most dangerous hazards for poultry farmers. Chickens' optimum productivity depends on a stable temperature range of between 99-102 °F with a relative humidity of 50-55% from 1-17 days, rising to 70% from 18-21 days (Liverpool-Tasie et al., 2019).

An increase in global warming has a direct effect on maize production, which indirectly influences poultry production. Though maize is a significant component of most poultry and livestock feed, lower maize yields and price fluctuations directly affect poultry productivity levels (Liverpool-Tasie et al., 2019).

Generally, most chickens cope well in typically hot and cold weather. It's only when there are extreme highs and drops in temperature that you need to worry about the birds' well-being.

Excessive Heat

Increased temperatures on poultry more often than not result in a marked reduction in egg laying. Broilers may lose valuable fatty tissue due to drinking more water and eating less grain. Poultry mortalities generally rise rapidly due to heat stress and inhibited immune response.

Increased Cold

The reason so many birds migrate is to avoid the cold so that their species may survive to continue breeding in the warmer climates of the world. As poultry can't escape the cold weather like their feathered cousins, this livestock relies on their keepers' intervention and care for their survival.

A severe drop in the temperature causes cold stress for poultry, resulting in the formation of gastrointestinal lesions and necrotic enteritis. This physical environmental stressor has the potential to decimate poultry stocks substantially.

PREPARE FOR THE FALL AND THE WINTER

Though raising chickens in winter can be a challenge, it can also be a lot of fun. Watching your hens' antics when they first encounter snow can be highly entertaining. There's no need to worry overly about the hens catching a chill. Their lovely, warm, and soft feathers beneath form a thick downy layer, which will keep your precious chickens quite snug and waterproof.

However, several important aspects of chicken rearing that you should keep in mind as the weather cools.

TIPS TO KEEP YOUR BROOD WARM IN THE WINTER

Despite the weather, your chickens are a lot tougher than you may think. They are, in fact, more likely to suffer from heatstroke in summer than die of cold in winter. Most chickens, especially those bred to tolerate the colder weather will cope well during the colder months.

There shouldn't be any need for added heat lamps, especially for smaller backyard flocks. A healthy chicken's body temperature is about 106 °F. As mentioned above, their feathery layers insulate the birds against the cold.

Your chickens generate a fair amount of body heat inside the coop and are likely to be quite cozy for most of the winter.

However, you may want to add a little extra insulation to the floor in the form of bedding material. Placing hay bales around the inner walls of the coop will also insulate it against the cold.

The only time you may need to step in to regulate the temperature is when the external ambient temperature drops below freezing. It's then not advisable to let your birds out of the coop until the weather conditions improve.

Keep the coop well-protected from draughts without sealing it. Adequate ventilation is still vital for the prevention of ammonia gas buildup.

WATCH OUT FOR FROZEN FEED AND WATER

When temperatures plummet, ensure your flock has an adequate supply of fresh lukewarm water. The feed should be dry and at room temperature. Substitute regular feed with options that won't freeze.

Keep a thermometer in the coop to gauge the temperature of the feed and water. Since the chickens need more food in winter to supply enough energy to maintain their body warmth, make sure there's enough feed for your flock.

Invest in commercially produced complete layer feeds that are nutrient-rich and suitable for your chickens' dietary needs during the colder months. The 90/10 rule will still apply in winter (See chapter three).

PREVENTING WATER FREEZING

Move waterers into the already-prepared winterized run, which should be warmer than the exterior ambient temperature.

Check and refill water containers throughout the day.

Insulate water containers with old tubing, bubble wrap, old towels, or straw.

REMOVE WET SPOTS

Check the coop out for wet spots and remove these immediately to avoid chickens getting chilled feet. Damp patches also tend to cause clumping and the potential for ammonia gas to build up, as already mentioned in chapter five.

INCREASE LIGHTING FOR EGG PRODUCTION

To maintain egg production, install an incandescent 25-watt bulb or LED3 to light 100 square feet of coop space. An automatic timer will allow you the freedom to be snug in your home while knowing your chickens have light in theirs. It'll also save you having to run back and forth to the coop to switch lights on and off during freezing weather.

WHAT TO FEED YOUR CHICKENS DURING THE WINTER MONTHS

Although some chicken keepers believe feeding chickens a little oatmeal during winter is beneficial, others don't agree. Oats contain some indigestible fiber that may cause your chickens' digestive tract to thicken, thus reducing the birds' ability to digest food and absorb essential nutrients properly.

Some keepers feed greens, and others believe dry feed is sufficient for their birds' needs. The challenge is to find out what food best suits your flock. You'll need to provide your birds with an essential balanced, organic diet of pellets, which should provide the necessary nutrients for your hens during winter. You may decide to add a little grain, cracked corn, and table scraps. Don't forget to give the birds grit and crushed oyster shells at intervals throughout the colder months.

ENCOURAGE EXPLORATION

As you'll no doubt know by now, chickens are busy, curious birds that love exploring. Whatever the weather, your flock will be stamping their feet to get outdoors where they can stretch their legs, necks, and wings.

> Chickens have a similar tendency as kids to become easily bored and then get into mischief. Chicken misbehavior can turn quite deadly, primarily if one chicken draws blood. To avoid "coop"-phobia, spend time with your brood in the winter. Walk and talk with your flock. The girls love to cuddle and

sometimes croon with pleasure when you snuggle them close and rub their heads with your chin.

For the most part, your flock can tolerate pretty chilly weather. The birds' blood supply to their feet and toes is sufficient to save these extremities from freezing. When chickens are on the move, they keep warm.

FUN AND GAMES

Chickens are naturally curious animals that love to poke their beaks into crevices as they hunt for tasty critters, bugs, and tidbits. To keep your flock occupied and challenge their intelligence, try one of the chicken games listed below.

Chicken Ball

A great idea to keep these feathered family members entertained during the cold months is to play "chicken ball." Collect a few sturdy small plastic containers into which you place some treats. Seal the containers and then poke several holes into the sides of the containers. The holes should be just the right size into which their beaks can slide. Shake the containers to draw your flock's attention before tossing them onto the ground.

The curious hens will want to investigate, and pretty soon, they'll figure out there are treats stashed inside. Using their ingenuity, those birds that are quicker at problem-solving will get the goodies. There will be members of the flock who are neither as quick nor intelligent, so you'll have to encourage them to play along with some extra treats to not miss out on the fun.

You may find treat balls for cats at your local pet store, which may work even better than the homemade option suggested above.

Chicken Rope Tug

Another challenging activity is the thread treats into spliced rope. The chickens will love pulling and tugging at the tidbits. The cords can be strung low enough for the hens to reach without jumping, or they can be laid out in different parts of the coop or run.

Chick Snatch

Tie small treats to different lengths of string which are then strung around the coop or the run. Watch your birds jump and flap to snatch the tasty treats. Their excitement and antics will have you laughing until your sides ache!

Cabbage Tetherball

Suspend a juicy cabbage from a hook where the chickens can peck away at the leaves and rip the vegetable to shreds. The birds love this activity as it keeps them occupied and offers a nice nutritious treat.

Treat Baskets

A similar idea to the tetherball, fill a small wire basket into which you place a disposable foil tray with a variety of small treats.

Suspend the basket in a spot where the chickens can reach in to inspect and gobble up the treasures you've left there.

You can use cooked corn, fruit, tasty berries and nuts, lettuce leaves, mealworms, grits, rice, sunflower seeds, or table scraps. See "Yummy Snacks" in chapter three.

COLLECT EGGS FREQUENTLY

The longer you leave eggs in the nesting boxes, the greater the chance these will freeze. There's no point in wasting perfect, fresh eggs by allowing them to crack and spoil.

If the coop temperature is below 45 °F and the eggs are cold to the touch, place them in the refrigerator to maintain the bloom so they don't spoil (DeannaCat, 2019).

Don't wash cold eggs, as this will also damage the bloom.

Fill the nesting boxes with dry, fresh straw and keep the containers clean. Remove any wet poop from the boxes immediately you spot it.

ENSURE THE COOP IS DRAFT-FREE

There's been a lot said about keeping the coop clean, dry, and ventilated, so what about draughts? Ventilation is essential for managing the removal of toxic gas. Strategically placed vents near the coop's roof, away from the nesting area, will help draw moist, warm air up and out of the enclosure without creating draughts of air.

However, the adequate movement of fresh air through the coop is very different from a draught. Draughts occur when small openings or cracks allow a chilly concentrated stream of air to filter directly into the coop. Draughts are sometimes tricky to manage and can cause chicken fatalities if left unattended.

Wrapping your coop in durable plastic sheeting works wonders for increasing the inside temperature by as much as 20 °F (DeannaCat, 2019).

Your chicken coop should already have a well-sealed, waterproof roof. If not, this task should become your priority!

PROVIDE A WELL-PROTECTED OUTDOOR SPACE

A winterized chicken run will make a safe, weatherproof, and sunny area filled with fresh air that your chickens can run, scratch, and only do outdoor chicken stuff in.

Polytunnels and homemade greenhouses work well. Draping durable plastic sheeting over the existing run will add protection and insulation against the icy winds.

Throw layers of straw onto the ground to give the chickens a more comfortable area on which to walk.

As soon as the birds return to the coop, dry their feet off well and inspect their toes and pads for frostbite.

THE DEEP LITTER METHOD

Already discussed at length in chapter five, the deep litter method generates its own warmth, which will help to keep your flock snug.

WATCH OUT FOR FROSTBITE

Good ventilation keeps the humidity level low, protecting your flock from suffering frostbite on their wattles, earlobes, and combs.

Chickens living in cold and damp conditions are more likely to suffer from this painful and sometimes irreversible condition. High windchill and excessive moisture cause condensation on the fragile comb and wattles. As the moisture cools and then freezes, frostbite occurs.

Signs of Frostbite
The first sign of frostbite will be darkened tips to the comb and wattles. Sometimes, discoloration of these areas and blistering occurs.

Treatment:
Make sure the coop is dry and warm, then lube your chickens' wattles, combs, and ear lobes with petroleum jelly or coconut oil to protect these sensitive areas against frostbite (DeannaCat, 2019).

THE BREED AND AGE OF YOUR FLOCK

Fully feathered adult chickens are more likely to cope with winter weather than younger birds that aren't yet fully feathered.

In some instances, younger chickens may need to be moved into your home during severe weather conditions. Just remember not to keep these birds too close to open fires or electric heating systems, as they may overheat.

The young birds should be kept in draught-proof containers that can be moved into sunny patches when these are available (DeannaCat, 2019).

Best Breeds for Winter
Although most chickens cope well during the winter months, several breeds are particularly winter-hardy. Among these are the Easter Eggers, Orpingtons, Ameraucana, Brahmas, and Australorps (DeannaCat, 2019).

MOLTING DURING WINTER

Most chickens go through their annual molt during the fall and have regained most of their new feather covering by the time winter hits. However, some chickens might be a little slow in gathering themselves together for the colder months and may need extra support. If your chickens look a little naked, you can try the following ideas (DeannaCat, 2019):

- Provide extra protein-rich feed for the slower feather growers.
- Make sure the sparsely clad birds are tucked between two fluffy chicken chums on the roost at night.
- If necessary, scantily clad birds may probably do betting in your home at night.
- Do NOT attempt to dress these birds in jumpers, as these garments are likely to cause them intense discomfort as they press against the newly forming feathers.

TIPS TO KEEP YOUR BROOD COOL IN SUMMER

For the most part, your chickens will enjoy summer almost as much as you. However, most chickens can overheat quite quickly when the ambient temperature rises. As a beginner chicken keeper, you should be aware that your birds will need plenty of hydration, good coop ventilation, and a complete, well-balanced chicken feed to keep them in excellent health during the hotter months of the year (Biggs, 2020).

Like you, your chickens also need shelter from the sun during summer. Since your chickens don't sweat, their cooling mechanism is to spread their wings to facilitate a better airflow around their bodies. Chickens will often pant when they're hot.

GOOD HYDRATION

Staying hydrated is essential for survival. You'll most likely agree you drink more fluids during summer than at any other time in the year. Briggs (2020) suggests a good rule of thumb for your hydration is to halve your body weight in pounds and drink the equivalent in fluid ounces.

Your chickens need about 500 milliliters or 17 fluid ounces of fresh, clean water per bird per day. Your flock's water intake equates to more or less one gallon of fresh water per day for seven adult birds (Briggs, 2020).

Inadequate hydration will negatively impact egg production. Here are some valuable suggestions to hydrate your feathered family:

- Increase the number of waterers.
- Place waterers in shady areas.
- Add ice cubes to the waterers to keep the water temperature cool.
- Place marbles or similar sized pebbles in the waterers to reduce splashing.
- Offer your flock cool, fresh, clean water morning and evening.
- Disinfect waterers weekly with a 1:10 bleach solution.

BODY TEMPERATURE

Your chickens' body temperature should be 105–107 °F. A rise in body temperature leads to heat stress, seizures, and even death. Keep your chickens cool in the following ways:

- Provide lots of shaded areas for your birds.
- Spray the birds regularly or encourage them to run under the garden sprinkler.
- Ensure the birds have good ventilation in the coop as well as the chicken run.
- Switch off all lights in the coop during summer.
- Exchange solid coop doors for fly screen mesh.
- Avoid overcrowding.

FEEDING CHICKENS IN SUMMER

Chickens can suffer from summertime blues, so you must supply them a healthy balanced diet with added fresh fruits, vegetables, and tasty snacks like watermelon, which is often a great favorite for chickens! However, don't forget the 90/10 rule.

Supply your birds with a good quality complete chicken feed twice daily.

Offer treats only once the feed is finished. These snacks can take the form of cold or frozen fruits and vegetables.

Offer crushed oyster shells to keep the birds' calcium intake high and include grits.

Don't force-feed your chickens, as they'll automatically eat less during the summer months.

CARING FOR CHICKENS IN EXTREME WEATHER

Sometimes, the weather can turn unusually nasty, and it's at these unexpected times you need to have a plan at the back of your mind to protect your chickens against harm.

As a beginner chicken keeper, you may have experienced any number of challenging weather conditions. Still, now you have the added concern of your small flock of chickens to protect against the harsh elements.

Violent storms and severe weather conditions worldwide kill more people every year than you may imagine. No matter how much you worry about your flock, your first responsibility will be to your family.

That said, if you live in an area where storms and extreme weather are part and parcel of your life, you'll have made plans already for the protection of your family, pets, and chickens.

However, it's those unexpected weather changes that cause the most concern; as with all things, preparation is vital for survival.

HURRICANES AND TORNADOES

You'll usually have prior warning of these events, and you'll need to exercise your common sense and not panic. Though you may have made adequate provision for your family and other pets, you now have the added responsibility of a small flock of helpless chickens that depend entirely on you for their safety and survival.

If you live in a tornado and hurricane belt, you'll probably have a bunker or safe place ready and prepared with provisions, bedding, clothing, a first aid kit, utensils, tools, and dozens of other essential items.

As soon as you're under a tornado warning, grab your family, weather radio, books, blankets, cell phones, and chargers, and get to your safe place. Ensure that among your extra supplies are LED lights, batteries, matches and firelighters, gas, and some sort of heating and cooling equipment.

Tornadoes are somewhat of a challenge, as these natural phenomena arise suddenly. Unlike hurricanes, tornadoes have a set path through which they move. Destructive and dangerous as they are, your coop is unlikely to be directly in the tornado's path (Anger, 2015).

On the other hand, hurricanes move through a vast area taking everything moveable with them as they roar over sections of land.

Depending on the time you have to get your family to safety, which will be your priority, here are some potentially useful ideas for your chickens' survival.

Chicken Survival

Once your family is safe and secure, and if you have time to move your flock to your safe place, consider an easily portable cage with an old broom handle that will double as a perch and a carrying handle. Grab extra bedding, feed, water, and a waterproof sheet in readiness for your small flock, and move the cage to your safe place. Chickens, like most pets, are easily unnerved by violent weather changes, so it's crucial to have the birds with you for their added comfort and reassurance.

Some chicken keepers in these situations have ready-made chicken runs erected in their safe place for just such eventualities. An old camping tent can form a functional, safe space for your flock.

However, if your coop is a solid structure that can withstand the wind force, board up the windows just as you'd do for your home. Secure the ventilation vent facing the oncoming storm and leave plenty of food and water for your birds if you can't get directly back to them after the hurricane has passed.

Though unlikely to withstand the force of hurricane winds, your hens' movable coop should be moved away from trees closer to a wall that may offer some protection.

Cover the coop securely with weatherproof sheeting or a tarp. Pay special attention to ensuring the coop's sides are protected against the horizontal wind and rain that characterizes this type of weather condition.

Once the storm has passed, inspect your chickens' structure and remove the tarp so that the birds can breathe easier. In all likelihood, the birds will snuggle together in the safest part of the coop and may survive the storm (Anger, 2015).

THUNDERSTORMS AND FLOODING

Sudden, severe rainstorms can cause unexpected flooding, which can be devastating to people and pets. The frightening thing about these natural disasters is that you usually have no control over how they play out.

Roads, bridges, and dwellings can be washed away, and sadly, many animals are drowned.

Frightening though it may be, if you live in a potential floodplain, obtain a flood area map that will help you plan an evacuation procedure for your family and animals in case of flooding.

In the event of a flash flood, you're unlikely to have time to gather your family and pets, so your best option is to consider leaving the coop open so that your birds at least have a chance to fly to higher ground if they can (Holloway, 2021)

The Aftermath

Cleaning up after heavy rains and flooding is devastating and, in many cases, heartbreaking. However, you may be fortunate enough to salvage valuable items to rebuild your coop. Sanitize these items and allow them to dry completely before reuse.

The greatest challenge after an event of this nature isn't only the water damage but the real chance of waterborne diseases and dangerous toxins (Holloway, 2021).

If you have time to prepare, containers of fresh, clean water will become lifesavers!

THE PARTING SHOT

Having weathered the inclement weather conditions as a rookie chicken keeper, you now get to pat yourself on the back and enjoy that great feeling of wallowing in your success. Good job. All your fellow backyard chicken keepers are rooting for you, too!

It's time to get down to the nitty-gritty of egg laying and learn how to improve your chicken keeping techniques to up your flock's productivity.

8. LAYING HENS AND EGG PRODUCTION

Egg collection is perhaps the most exciting part of being a beginner backyard chicken keeper. You need some basic knowledge about egg production and collection and what it takes to improve the quality and quantity of eggs.

Without further ado, let's get into the groove to discover more about how backyard chickens can provide you with the best eggs ever!

WHAT TO EXPECT

Each hen can lay one egg per day, though not every hen will lay an egg every day. With this in mind, you need to know what to expect from your hens.

Jacob (n.d.-b) says the laying cycle is influenced by the hen's exposure to light. The first will often be laid early in the morning. An egg takes about 26 hours to form inside the hen's reproductive tract after the last egg was laid. This fact means that each hen will lay an egg later each day than the day before. Eventually, the hen will lay an egg too late in the day for a new egg to begin forming. The hen will then miss a day of laying before she gets back into the laying cycle again.

The hens in your flock are unlikely to all lay at the same time, so laying will happen throughout the day, depending on each hen's individual laying cycle.

In an egg production graph, you'll notice the production peaks and then gradually diminishes over about 20 to 75 weeks of age. Some backyard flocks will produce eggs for up to four years, with the egg production level dropping each year slightly (Jacob, n.d.-b).

As your flock ages, egg production will decrease. However, the rate at which this process occurs depends on the following factors.

Breed

Some birds are bred to be more prolific layers than others. The Leghorn lays white eggs. Rhode Island Reds produce brown eggs, and a mixed-breed flock will supply both brown and white eggs.

Pullet Management

If your chickens have enjoyed a good start, had a well-balanced diet, plenty of fresh, clean water, adequate space to move around, and a cozy, safe coop, there's no reason they shouldn't give you plenty of eggs.

The health of your pullets is, of course, an essential factor in the egg production process.

Light Exposure

As mentioned, light stimulates your hens to lay. If your flock has enjoyed a healthy outdoor life and is exposed to laying lights after dark, these hens will likely lay more eggs than other birds without the added lighting.

Light stimulation has proved helpful in increasing egg production; chickens are known to be "long-season breeders," says Jacob (n.d.-b)

Healthy Diet and Nutrition

Chapter three discussed the vital importance of good nutrition for your flock. Birds raised on a well-balanced diet of the correct feed should become proficient layers. A calcium-rich diet will ensure laying hens produce good quality eggs.

Space

Adequate space is needed for laying hens to produce effectively. Egg production in overcrowded hen houses is likely to drop off quicker than in a smaller, more spacious backyard coop. Hens with enough perching space will lay more prolifically than those without (Jacob, n.d.-b).

HOW TO IDENTIFY LAYING HENS

Jacob (n.d.-b) recommends the better your understanding of the breed, the more likely you'll be to identify when these birds are ready to lay. For some breeds, laying hens display their bright red comb and wattles.

For hens with yellow pigments like the Rhode Island Reds, the pigmentation gradually fades from vent to the beak, face, and then the legs.

Another method is to judge the increased size of the hen's abdominal area. The larger the abdomen, the more likely the hen is getting ready to lay.

Laying hens often become broody. They'll often scratch and fuss in the nesting box or find another suitable spot they feel comfortable to lay.

REASONS WHY HENS MAY NOT LAY

Distressing as it is when your hens don't lay, there are several reasons this may happen.

Hens Have Reached the End of Their Laying Cycle

Most hens take a break from laying after about 10 months. These birds will molt and rest for a month or more before they start laying again.

If your hens lay for less than 10 months, there may be another underlying issue causing a decline in their production.

Insufficient Fresh, Clean Water

Are you aware that your hens won't eat if they don't have sufficient water to drink? A constant supply of fresh, clean water is paramount to the hens' health and egg production.

Poor Quality Feed or a Dietary Imbalance

Poor diet, insufficient good-quality feed, or limited ratios will adversely affect egg production.

Decreased Light Hours

Egg production is directly linked to light hours. A decrease in light and the absence of additional light will ensure a reduction in egg production.

Parasitic Infestation

Both internal parasites such as worms, and **Coccidia protozoa**, in addition to external parasites such as mites, fleas, and lice can cause your hens to stop egg production.

Effective treatment of these infestations should be swift to overcome the problem and get your hens back on the egg-laying track.

Diseased Birds

Poultry can suffer from many debilitating diseases which affect the respiratory, digestive, immune, reproductive, and nervous systems. Some disorders cause paralysis, skin ailments, and metabolic disturbances.

It's challenging to know if your hens are suffering from any of these diseases. If you suspect one of your birds is unwell, seek immediate advice from your backyard chicken support group, or take the hen to the nearest avian veterinarian (Jacob, n.d.-b).

THE JOY OF COLLECTING EGGS

After all your endeavors to give your chickens the best care possible, these delightful birds have rewarded you with fresh eggs. How amazing! The first time you collect eggs from your hens will be imprinted on your memory forever.

Here are four crucial tips to ensure the eggs are correctly handled, washed, and stored.

Keep Nesting Boxes Clean

Ensure that the nesting boxes are always clean with fresh linings, and remove any poop from the box when you collect the eggs.

Collect Eggs Daily

Make sure to collect eggs daily to avoid unnecessary breakages and chickens eating their eggs.

Cleaning Eggs

The process of cleaning these fragile items is essential for presenting healthy, germ-free eggs for your family and customers. Check on the state laws before selling your eggs (Arcuri, 2020a).

On occasion, the wet-cleaning method may be used when

the egg has stains, yolk splashes, or wet muck attached. Wash the eggs carefully under warm, running water and dry well. Spray the eggs with a dilution of water and a little bleach.

The dry-cleaning method is preferable as the bloom (natural antibacterial layer) on the egg remains intact. Gently rub the shell with a dry sponge to remove any dirt or poop.

Packing and Storing Eggs
Pack clean eggs into date stamped cartons reflecting the day on which the eggs were collected. Refrigeration is always best for extended keeping. Eggs are usually good for four to six weeks refrigerated. Eggs at room temperature are perfect for daily use.

Egg Freshness Test
Eggs that float in water have accumulated air, which means that their contents are likely to have deteriorated (Arcuri, 2020a).

GOLDEN TIPS FOR QUALITY EGGS

Now comes more excitement! Here are more valuable tips to improve your hens' laying capacity and, in turn, increase their egg production.

Quality chicken care starts from the day you bring your chickens home to their new roost. During these early days and months, you lay the foundation for the eventual successful egg production you want to achieve (Roeder, 2021).

High-Quality Laying Feed
When you come to think about it, egg laying is a full-time job for your hens. Thus, we should provide the birds with premium, high-quality laying feed from as early as 18 weeks. There are several excellent commercial feeds on the market from which to choose.

Complete layer feeds comprise a balance of essential nutrients, vitamins, minerals, prebiotics, probiotics, and calcium for optimum egg quality and hen health. The full laying feed should comprise 90% of your hens' diet. The remaining 10% can be additional components such as table scraps, crushed oyster shells, and scratch grain. The 90/10 balance is crucial for the best egg quality and production!

Collect Eggs Regularly
As already mentioned, regular egg collection (two or three times per day) is essential for cleaner eggs with less chance of cracking and damage. Bacteria easily infiltrate cracked eggs which will result in the egg being spoiled.

Cracked eggs are more easily broken when hens move around the nest. Once a curious hen has spotted a leaking egg, they'll likely peck at it out of interest. When the hen discovers this tasty treat, she may figure out that pecking other eggs will give her the same delicious meal. In no time, eggs will begin to disappear, and productivity will wane as a result.

Increase Light
As you've already learned, light is essential for egg production. By increasing the light to about 17 hours daily, the natural hormonal response to lying is increased. A single incandescent 25-watt or LED3 (up to LED8) bulb will give sufficient light to prompt your hens to lay regularly.

As with all backyard chicken keeping, routine and consistent good management will reap the rewards you hoped for.

CONCLUSION

Now that you have a solid foundation for raising backyard chickens, you're ready to engage in the poultry industry. You're no longer an overly anxious beginner backyard chicken breeder. You've reached the point where you have the confidence to work with your precious flock and provide these amazingly productive and endearing birds with the best food and every comfort they need.

You'll have discovered your chickens are hardier and more resilient than you may have first believed. The birds are pretty good at taking care of themselves, provided you've supplied them with adequate quality feed, plenty of fresh, clean water, and secure living quarters.

The less crowded your birds, the better their temperament will be and the fewer their behavioral problems. Though some hens can be fussy and others adorable and affectionate, caring for the unique characters in your flock is part of the fun of raising a backyard brood.

Where before being a chicken keeper, you may now have a fully equipped poultry sick bay, which has possibly become part and parcel of your daily chicken care routine. Plus, you're most likely very proud of the fact that you can now service some of the more basic health needs of your flock.

Finally, there's little doubt that you'll have discovered backyard chicken keeping is an addictive hobby! So, without further ado, good luck with your continued chicken keeping. Life will never be boring while you have these delightful gals to enrich each day with their humorous antics and their utterly entertaining and gratifying presence in your life.

PLEA FROM THE AUTHOR

I hope you enjoyed the book and found it an informative and useful read. I will very much appreciate if you can let me and others know your level of satisfaction by leaving a review.

You can log into your amazon account or go to:

amazon.com/ryp

REFERENCES

5M Editor. (2009, January 6). In-House windrow composting Q and A. Www.thepoultrysite.com. https://www.thepoultrysite.com/articles/inhouse-windrow-composting-q-and-a.

5M Editor. (2005, January 31). Avian Influenza in poultry. Www.thepoultrysite.com. https://www.thepoultrysite.com/articles/avian-influenza-in-poultry.

Admin, A. (2019, February 28). Protecting your chickens from Newcastle Disease. Freedom Ranger Blog. https://www.freedomrangerhatchery.com/blog/protecting-your-chickens-from-newcastle-disease/.

Agriculture.com Staff. (2018, January 6). Feeding medicated chicken feeds. Successful Farming. https://www.agriculture.com/livestock/poultry/feed/medicated-chicken-feeds_292-ar13577.

All images are courtesy of Pixabay and Shutterstock

Anger, R. H. (2015, September 2). Preparing the flock for hurricanes and tornadoes. Hobby Farms. https://www.hobbyfarms.com/preparing-the-flock-for-hurricanes-and-tornadoes/#:~:text=You%20can%20cover%20a%20fixed.

Arcuri L. (2012). What should I feed my chickens? The Spruce. https://www.thespruce.com/feeding-your-chickens-or-laying-hens-3016556.

Arcuri L. (2020, January 12). Easy chicken care for your small farm. The Spruce. https://www.thespruce.com/daily-and-monthly-chicken-care-tasks-3016823.

Arcuri, L. (2020a, July 21). Tips for collecting and cleaning chicken eggs. The Spruce. https://www.thespruce.com/collect-clean-and-store-chicken-eggs-3016828.

Banrie. (2012, December 17). Poultry litter management. Www.thepoultrysite.com. https://www.thepoultrysite.com/articles/poultry-litter-management.

Beautyofbirds. (2020). Fowl Cholera | Beauty of Birds. Www.beautyofbirds.com. https://www.beautyofbirds.com/fowlcholera.html.

Bentoli. (2017, August 15). Six common chicken problems you can fight with proper nutrients | Bentoli. Bentoli. https://www.bentoli.com/chicken-problems-common/.

Biggs, P. (2020). How to keep chickens cool in the summertime. Purina Animal Nutrition. https://www.purinamills.com/chicken-feed/education/detail/summer-flock-care-how-to-keep-chickens-cool.

Chelsea Green Publishing. (2020, March 6). Manage your chicken manure: The joys of deep litter | Chelsea Green Publishing. Www.chelseagreen.com. https://www.chelseagreen.com/2020/manage-your-chicken-manure-deep-litter/.

Claire. (2015, June 3). 7 Surprising rules for feeding chickens. Thehappychickencoop.com. https://www.thehappychickencoop.com/7-surprising-rules-for-feeding-chickens/.

CuzChickens. (2016). Wound care for chickens. Backyard Chickens. https://www.backyardchickens.com/articles/wound-care-for-chickens.72385/.

DeannaCat. (2019, November 14). 10 Tips on caring for chickens in cold winter weather. Homestead and Chill. https://homesteadandchill.com/caring-for-chickens-in-winter/.

Esmail, S. H. (2011, October 25). Litter management – Part 1: Good litter for healthy birds. PoultryWorld. https://www.poultryworld.net/Broilers/Housing/2011/10/Litter-management--Part-1-Good-litter-for-healthy-birds-WP009463W/.

Farm & Pet Place. (2016, May 3). Organic chicken feed - A complete guide.. Farm & Pet Place Blog. https://www.farmandpetplace.co.uk/blog/organic-chicken-feed-a-complete-guide/#:~:text=Lower%20risk%20of%20bad%20health.

Fox, G., & Fox, K. (2018, March 23). Coccidiosis & your chickens - What you need to know. Freedom Ranger Hatchery. https://www.freedomrangerhatchery.com/blog/coccidiosis-your-chickens-what-you-need-to-know/#:~:text=The%20most%20popular%20treatment%20for.

Frame, D. (2010). Basics for raising backyard chickens. https://cpif.org/wp-content/uploads/2014/06/Basics-for-Raising-

Backyard-Chickens-copy-3.pdf.

Guest. (2017, February 14). 7 Best chicken tips for first-time chicken owners. Common Sense Home. https://commonsensehome.com/best-chicken-tips/.

Holloway, L. (2021). How to prepare your chicken coop for severe weather. PetHelpful. https://pethelpful.com/farm-pets/Preparing-Your-Coop-for-Severe-Weather.

Jacob, J. (n.d.). Normal Behaviors of chickens in small and backyard poultry flocks – Small and backyard poultry. Poultry.extension.org. https://poultry.extension.org/articles/poultry-behavior/normal-behaviors-of-chickens-in-small-and-backyard-poultry-flocks/.

Jacob, J. (n.d.-b). Raising chickens for egg production – Small and backyard poultry. Poultry.extension.org. https://poultry.extension.org/articles/poultry-management/raising-chickens-for-egg-production/.

Johnson, R. (2018, May 24). The importance of lighting in poultry production. Www.thepoultrysite.com. https://www.thepoultrysite.com/articles/the-importance-of-lighting-in-poultry-production.

Johnston, C. (2018, September 24). How to start raising backyard chickens in 7 simple steps. Wholefully. https://wholefully.com/how-to-start-raising-backyard-chickens-in-7-simple-steps/.

Katherine. (2019, May 9). Top benefits of raising and keeping backyard chickens. Dogwood Pond Farms. https://www.dogwoodpondfarms.com/benefits-of-raising-backyard-chickens/.

Kathy, T. C. C. (n.d.). Fowl Pox prevention & treatment | The Chicken Chick®. The Chicken Chick. https://the-chicken-chick.com/fowl-pox-prevention-treatmen/.

Lesley, C. (2020a, May 4). The definitive guide to egg laying problems | Chickens And More. Chickens and More. https://www.chickensandmore.com/egg-laying-problems/#:~:text=Sometimes%20 hens%20will%20stop%20laying.

Lesley, C. (2020b, August 2). Common chicken health problems. Old Farmer's Almanac. https://www.almanac.com/common-chicken-health-problems#.

Lesley, C. (2020c, September 28). Dominique chicken, all you need to know: Temperament and egg-laying | Chickens And More. Chickens and More. https://www.chickensandmore.com/dominique-chicken/.

Linden, J. (2015, February 13). Nutrition for the backyard flock. Www.thepoultrysite.com. https://www.thepoultrysite.com/articles/nutrition-for-the-backyard-flock.

Liverpool-Tasie, L. S. O., Sanou, A., & Tambo, J. A. (2019). Climate change adaptation among poultry farmers: evidence from Nigeria. Climatic Change, https://doi.org/10.1007/s10584-019-02574-8(December 2019). https://doi.org/10.1007/s10584-019-02574-8.

LLC, A. (2021). Salmonellosis in chickens. PoultryDVM. http://www.poultrydvm.com/condition/salmonellosis.

Manitoba. (1945, June). Agriculture | Province of Manitoba. Province of Manitoba - Agriculture. https://www.gov.mb.ca/agriculture/livestock/production/poultry/poultry-rations-and-feeding-methods.html#:~:text=In%20any%20case%20 the%20flock.

McMurray Staff. (2017, May 11). Safe table scraps for your chickens | McMurray Hatchery Blog. McMurray Hatchery Blog. https://blog.mcmurrayhatchery.com/2017/05/11/safe-table-scraps-chickens/.

Melissa. (2012, July 5). Caring for your flock on a daily, weekly, monthly and seasonal basis. Tilly's Nest. https://www.tillysnest.com/2012/07/caring-for-your-flock-on-daily-weekly-html/.

Mormino, K. S. (2012a, April 5). Droppings boards, because poop happens | The Chicken Chick®. The-Chicken-Chick.com. https://the-chicken-chick.com/droppings-boards-because-poop-happens/.

Mormino, K. S. (2012, July 8). Chicken heat stress, dehydration, and homemade electrolyte solution | The Chicken Chick®. The-Chicken-Chick.com. https://the-chicken-chick.com/chicken-heat-stress-dehydration-and/.

Mormino, K. S. (2013, July 4). 11+ Tips for predator-proofing chickens | The Chicken Chick®. The-Chicken-Chick.com. https://the-chicken-chick.com/11-tips-for-predator-proofing-chickens/.

Neyens, D. (2019, February 25). Caring for chickens in extreme weather. Counting My Chickens. http://www.countingmychickens.com/caring-for-chickens-in-extreme-weather/.

Omlet. (2004). State laws concerning backyard chickens | Laws about keeping chickens | Chickens | Guide | Omlet US. Www.omlet.us. https://www.omlet.us/guide/chickens/laws_about_keeping_chickens/

state_laws.

Poultry Care. (2019, February 7). Backyard chickens - Caring and raising your flock - Grange Co-op. Grange Co-Op. http://www.grangecoop.com/pros-cons-raising-backyard-chickens/.

Price, J. (2014, July 11). Raising backyard chickens for dummies. Modern Farmer. https://modernfarmer.com/2014/07/raising-backyard-chickens-dummies/.

Purina Animal Nutrition. (n.d.). How to start raising chickens. Purina Animal Nutrition. https://www.purinamills.com/chicken-feed/education/detail/steps-on-how-to-start-raising-chickens.

Purina. (2019). How to care for chickens in winter. Purina Animal Nutrition. https://www.purinamills.com/chicken-feed/education/detail/tips-for-raising-chickens-in-winter#:~:text=Chickens%2C%20especially%20cold%2Dtolerant%20breeds.

Ridgerunner. (2015, January 24). How much room do chickens need? Backyard Chickens - Learn how to raise chickens. https://www.backyardchickens.com/articles/how-much-room-do-chickens-need.66180/.

Roeder, M. (2021). Tips for quality eggs. Purina Animal Nutrition. https://www.purinamills.com/chicken-feed/education/detail/three-tips-to-help-your-hens-produce-quality-eggs.

Smith, K. (2020, June 26). Top 20 chicken breeds for your backyard coop. Backyard Chicken Coops. https://www.backyardchickencoops.com.au/blogs/learning-centre/top-20-chicken-breeds-for-your-backyard-coop.

Smith, K. (2020a, July 16). When will my chickens start laying eggs? Backyard Chicken Coops. https://www.backyardchickencoops.com.au/blogs/learning-centre/when-will-my-chickens-start-laying-eggs.

Smith, K. (2020b, July 22). The key to a deep chicken litter system. Backyard Chicken Coops. https://www.backyardchickencoops.com.au/blogs/learning-centre/the-key-to-a-deep-chicken-litter-system.

Star Milling. (2020). Breeds of chickens - Get the facts before you start your flock. Star Milling Co. https://starmilling.com/poultry-chicken-breeds/.

Steele, L. (2017). My top tips for keeping chickens when you work all day. Fresh Eggs Daily. https://www.fresheggsdaily.blog/2017/01/my-top-tips-for-keeping-chickens-when.html.

Telkamp, M. (2019). Notification. Hgtv.com. https://www.hgtv.com/outdoors/gardens/animals-and-wildlife/what-do-chickens-eat.

The Happy Chicken Coop. (2015, May 25). 5 Reasons to keep chickens. Thehappychickencoop.com. https://www.thehappychickencoop.com/5-reasons-to-keep-chickens/.

Urquhart, C. M. (2016, May 2). About raising chickens. Hobby Farms. https://www.hobbyfarms.com/about-raising-chickens/.

Walker, J. (2017, April 6). The chicken care tasks of poultry farmers. Coops and Cages. https://www.coopsandcages.com.au/blog/chicken-care-tasks-poultry-farmers/.

Whisperer, C. (2018). Benefits and challenges of raising chickens in urban areas. Www.chickenwhisperermagazine.com. https://www.chickenwhisperermagazine.com/the-chicken-movement/benefits-challenges-of-raising-chickens-in-urban-areas.

Williams, L. (2020, September 10). Prevent contaminated water with automated drinking systems. Www.thepoultrysite.com. https://www.thepoultrysite.com/articles/prevent-contaminated-water-with-automated-drinking-systems.

www.ingramcontent.com/pod-product-compliance
Ingram Content Group UK Ltd.
Pitfield, Milton Keynes, MK11 3LW, UK
UKHW041301180426
11947UKWH00009B/608

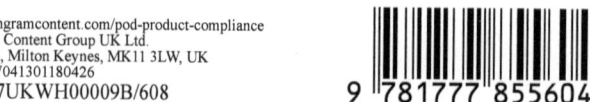